To Be a Man

D1602365

TO BE A MAN

Life Lessons
for Young Men

by James B. Stenson

 Scepter

Other books by James B. Stenson, published by Scepter Publishers

Lifeline: The Religious Upbringing of Your Children

Preparing for Adolescence: A Planning Guide for Parents

Preparing for Peer Pressure: A Guide for Parents of Young Children

*Successful Fathers: The Subtle but Powerful Ways Fathers Mold
    Their Children's Characters*

Upbringing: A Discussion Handbook for Parents of Young Children

Anchor: God's Promises of Hope to Parents

Compass: A Handbook on Parent Leadership

Father, the Family Protector

To Be a Man: Life Lessons for Young Men
Copyright © 2011 James B. Stenson.

Second printing, September 2012

ISBN 978-1-59417-162-8

Published by Scepter Publishers, Inc.
(800) 322–8773 / www.scepterpublishers.org

Contents

CHAPTER 1

The Big Picture

Because you're a busy young man, I'll get right to the point and explain what this small book is all about and why I wrote it for you.

This collection of notes is written for men mid-twenties and younger who want—and probably need—to profit from the experiences of people who've lived an active, productive life.

It deals with some of those issues important to a young man as he sets the course of his life as a working professional and head of a family—the overriding importance of strong character; making the most of one's education; finding what you're good at and then planning a career; preparing for marriage, living as a loving and supportive husband and father; acquiring social graces; dealing with friends; sizing up people; overcoming worries; standards of professionalism and professional etiquette; setting priorities and managing time; knowing nonsense when you see it; living as a responsible and engaged citizen; and enriching one's spiritual life—which is the power that holds everything else together.

Simply put, these notes of experience are really aimed at helping you find what we all seek in life—happiness.

Joseph Addison, an eighteenth-century English essayist, wisely said that there are three components to happiness—something to *do*, something to *love*, and something to *hope for*.

"Something to do" means meaningful work, putting our powers up against problems for the sake of others' welfare.

"Something to love" means an object for our hearts, for our capacity of sacrificial giving of self—family, friends, country, God.

"Something to hope for" means our spiritual values, our trust in God's help, our religious faith projected into the future.

Work, love, and faith are thus the secrets to happiness.

So the contents of this book are dedicated to helping you give greater life to, and thereby find greater happiness in, your work, your love for family and friends, and your interior life of friendship with God.

To look at the matter another way, youth is a crucially important time of life that should be thought out carefully, though it seldom is. What happens in the years of youth—ages sixteen to twenty-five, let's say—has deep and lasting influence. The habits you form, the friends you make, and the ideas and ideals you internalize—all these have lifelong consequences.

This is why there's a tradition in Western history of teacher-mentors assembling notes of experience—words of shrewdness, encouragement, wisdom, and savvy—to firm up the judgment and conscience of young men just setting out in life. For example, Baltazar Gracian's thoughts graced *The Art of Worldly Wisdom*. Castigione published *The Courtier* for young men of his day. St. Josemaría Escrivá composed *The Way* for students and young workers whom he befriended and led in spiritual direction.

This brief book of mine follows their example. It's my

hope that you will learn from these comments, all gleaned from people's experience in a host of situations, about the contours of a life well lived.

An American philosopher once defined wisdom as "the art of knowing what to ignore." He meant discerning what's important from what's not in a host of situations. It is my hope that you will grow in wisdom by learning from the experience of others set out in these pages.

You should not wait for a crisis to determine what's really important to you. If you set your principles firmly in place now, while you are young, your life will be confident and therefore joyful, active, and effective. It's easy to make decisions and stick with them when you know what your principles are. For people without principles, life is always complicated.

What sort of savvy advice am I talking about? Here are a few examples of what follows in this book, all taken from people's experience:

- Your personal integrity is your greatest asset. The word integrity is related to the word "integer," which denotes some sort of unity. So integrity means unity, but unity of what? Of three things: intention, word, and action. You mean what you say, you say what you mean, and you keep your word. In other words, you consistently tell the truth and you follow through on your promises. This commitment to truth and honor is absolutely essential to a clean conscience, a healthy marriage, and a successful career, no matter what you do for a living.

- Tedium is part of life. Most really important achievements—moving up in a career, forming a stable family life, mastering some skill—involve stretches of repetitive and apparently nonproductive action. Having a great goal or ideal is what turns drudgery into an adventurous and sporting pursuit.

- Love isn't just a bundle of sweet sentiments. Real love means sacrifice. It means taking on responsibility. Real love is the willingness and the capacity to undergo difficulties, hardship, setbacks, tedium, disappointments—all for the sake of someone else's welfare and happiness. This love is lived every day by conscientious parents, dedicated clergy, and those in the military who have sacrificed for our country.

- If you are thinking seriously of marrying someone, you should take a long, close look at the way she treats her family. Is she affectionate with them? Is she loyal to them, grateful, and generous? Or on the other hand, does she treat them with self-centered spite, resentment, ingratitude, and indifference? (Remember: the opposite of love isn't hatred; the opposite of love is indifference.) Pay close attention to all these attitudes, good and bad, because that's probably the way she will treat her husband.

- Don't ever "pad" or otherwise lie on your résumé. The one thing any company will fire you for on the spot, even years later, is the discovery that you've lied on your résumé.

- In professional life, dress for the job you want, not the one you have. Your bosses will notice.

- Contrary to popular mythology, you don't grow up when you can take care of yourself. Any animal can do this. You really grow up when you can take care of others—and want to. That's why maturity means responsibility. And responsibility is another term for love.

■   ■   ■

Life is short. As a Russian proverb says, "We pass through life like a knife through water." Life's passage is brief and turbulent, and it leaves only a fleeting wake; it's over quickly, and most people leave no trace behind them. Your life should not be like this. Your life should have savor, purpose, meaning. This book will, I hope, show you how to live the life God wants for you, a life of rich adventure.

Let us start by considering the all-important subject of *character*.

CHAPTER 2

Character: A Working Description

All the ideas and observations about life in this handbook have something to do with a man's character. They derive from the workings of sound character. What's more, they form and strengthen character.

This invisible thing we call character resides in a man's mind and will and heart. Like other spiritual qualities we esteem in people—such as healthy self-confidence, charisma, kindness, honesty, courage, willpower, "class" —character is hard to define but easy to detect. We recognize character when we see it in those around us, and we grow distressed, or at least uneasy, when it is missing, especially among people we must depend on.

Let's look at some commonsense descriptions of character; then we can focus in with a precise definition.

- Character is what we have left over if we ever go broke. Character is what each of us is, minus our money and possessions.

- Character is the aggregate of qualities that people esteem in us despite our flaws. Indeed, it's what they admire about us in how we cope with those flaws. (For instance, we respect someone who admits he's a "recovering alcoholic" and struggles to overcome his affliction.)

- Character is what people admire in us besides our talents and acquired skills. As we know, people may display dazzling talents and skills but still lack character. (Just read the sports page and see the glaring personal flaws of gifted athletes. Or glance around your workplace: the business world suffers no shortage of what might be called "technically skilled barbarians.")

- Character is what parents seek most in their grown children's prospective spouses. It's what parents want above all in their sons-in-law and daughters-in-law. The prospect of having a son or daughter marry someone without character is every conscientious parent's nightmare.

- Character is what employers hunt for when they read between the lines of job applicants' résumés and references.

- Character is what makes people proud and delighted to count us as friends, not just acquaintances. It is what makes real friendships last a lifetime.

- Character is what children unconsciously imitate in their parents' lives. It is the compass they take through life by which they judge their own peers, including prospective spouses.

Because character is an elusive idea, we need some sort of framework to think about it, a sensible breakdown into parts we can study. Here's one framework that many young men have found helpful. It comes with a pedigree more than 2,000 years old, for it was originally devised by the ancient Greeks.

The Greeks had a lot to say about character. Removed as they were from our complex world of computers, mass media, and technological gadgets, they formed a clear, unsurpassed vision of human nature. Though the Greeks lived imperfect lives themselves, nonetheless the best of them thought deeply about ethics, goodness, beauty, and truth. We still turn to them for wisdom because they were so often insightful about human life.

To the greatest minds of antiquity, character is an integration of what they term the "virtues," those powers of mind and will and heart that are built up through repeated practice: *prudence, justice, fortitude,* and *temperance.* Character, to them, is the sum total of these habitual powers joined together in one's personality. It determines what we are at the center of our very self, our soul. And it directly affects how we go about living with others.

For the sake of clarity, let's consider the great virtues—that is, character strengths—in more modern-day, commonsense terms:

- Prudence is *sound judgment and conscience.*
- Justice is *a sense of responsibility and fair play.*
- Fortitude is *courage, persistence, "guts."*
- Temperance is *self-mastery, self-discipline, self-control.*

To these four classical concepts of virtue, we add the other, immensely important inner strength drawn from our Judeo-Christian ethic—*heart.* (The ancient Greeks were, in many ways, a heartless people.) It is *generosity, magnanimity, charity, a capacity for compassionate understanding,* and *forgiveness.* In religious terms, it is the virtues of faith, hope, and charity—that is, to love and serve God by loving and serving others, starting with family and friends and radiating out to others, all brothers and sisters under our heavenly Father.

All this being said, let's look more closely at the virtues and their implications for your life as a man. After all, if some day you are a father, you will have the awesome responsibility of forming strong character in your children. This is what a father does.

Sound judgment

How can we understand the power of sound judgment, of thinking like a mature, responsible adult? Here are some ways of looking at this strength:

- Fundamentally, sound judgment is the power of *discernment*. It's the *acquired ability to make distinctions*, especially the great distinctions in life—truth from falsehood, good from evil, right from wrong. On the moral plane—that is, in the interplay between rights and duties—it's our conscience.

    Related to this, judgment is the power to understand human nature and life experience: to tell what is important in life from what is not, what is important in people and what is not. We have good judgment when we have the power to weigh people's motivations, values, and priorities in life. This is the power to recognize the good, the true, and the beautiful in life and in other people—and to distinguish these from the evil, the false, and the sordid.

Someone once asked an Oxford professor what he thought was the purpose of education. His answer: "Why, it's so young people can recognize rubbish when they see it!" Not a bad definition. As a result of their upbringing, at home and in school and in the workplace, young people should recognize lies, propaganda, and phoniness of all sorts when they see these things.

- Sound judgment is also *shrewdness*. It's the ability to appreciate the good in people, to grasp what moves them most—their values and ideals. It's the power to size up people quickly and deeply, but without the desire to dominate them. Aristotle said (to paraphrase him) that a philosopher, someone who loves truth and goodness, combines shrewdness and good will. Someone who is both shrewd and good-willed has the essence of wisdom.

- Sound judgment is *the ability to foresee the probable consequences, both good and bad, of a projected course of action.* (Also of inaction, for neglecting to act in time also has a consequence, often disastrous.) It's the power to make realistic risk-assessments. It involves learning from one's mistakes and successes and those of others.

- Sound judgment also means a respect for learning and intellectual achievement. This is a cordial familiarity with the greatest achievements of the human spirit, those accomplishments of mind, will, heart, and body that inspire us and prove that humans are not mere beasts. All great art, it is said, makes us proud to be human. And great literature leads us to see life through others' eyes; it expands our vision, deepens our judgment, and liberates us from the bonds of the *local*, the *present*, and the *self*.

- *Conscience*, the moral dimension of sound judgment, is the framework for judging the right thing to do in a tangled situation. It tells us what we *ought* to do so that we live ethically, honorably, in friendship with God and at peace with others, respecting their rights and dignity and feelings. This power of conscience is not just a bundle of shapeless sentiments; it's a thoughtful understanding of good and evil, right and wrong, built up through a lifetime of learning, but especially during the years of childhood and young adulthood.

Responsibility

What is responsibility? The Greeks called it *justice* and said it meant giving others what is due to them. The word "duty" is related to "due"—a duty is something we owe to others because they have a right to it.

If any of the great virtues come naturally to us as children, it would seem to be this one. Children call it "fairness," and they have a powerful sense of what is fair. For this reason, you can usually correct kids effectively when you appeal to their sense of fairness, and wise parents explain correction to their children in terms of what's fair. This lays a solid ground for more complex lessons of ethics later in the children's lives, especially during adolescence.

This virtue of responsibility is rich with meanings:

- Responsibility means acting so as to respect the rights of others, including their right not to be offended. (Thus it overlaps with charity, that is, consideration for others' feelings.) *Because other people have rights, we have obligations.* My right to throw a punch stops short of someone else's face. I have a right to scribble a drawing, but not to smear graffiti on someone's wall. I have a right to stand in line, but not to butt in. I have a right to shop, but not to have others foot the bill. I have a right to speak my mind, but not to interrupt or intentionally offend someone. This is a very important point. The goal of moral development is to move from *self* to *others.*

- Responsibility is a *habit of doing our duties whether we feel like it or not.* In family life, it is sacrificial love. Love means shouldering and carrying out our family obligations: in family life, responsibility shows our love.

  And in the world of work, responsibility means professionalism—the power to perform at our best no matter how we feel. Real professionals carry out their responsibilities, perform their services as best they can, even when they don't feel like it. Headaches, personal concerns, emotional ups and downs—none of these things deter effective professionals from fulfilling their duties of service.

- Responsibility is *respect for rightful authority.* Authority means, among other things, the right to be obeyed. Please remember this when you're a father: Great parents may harbor doubts about many things in their children's upbringing, but they have no doubts about their rightful authority. Successful parents are confident of their authority. They take for granted, so to speak, that their children will respect and obey them. As a result, their children, over time, grow to have *confidence in their parents' self-confidence.*

To look at it another way, effective fathers and mothers see their parenthood as a kind of high office, like that of president or supreme court justice. Whoever bears the burden of responsible public office, regardless of personal shortcomings, has a right to be respected and obeyed. So, too, no matter what personal faults or self-doubts they may have, parents, by the very fact of their parenthood, have a right to their children's respectful cooperation.

- Responsibility also means *living with the consequences of our decisions and mistakes, including our neglect.* How many problems in our society derive from attempts to escape responsibility? Responsible people do not shift blame; they refuse to see themselves as victims. They admit their mistakes honestly and shoulder the consequences.

- Responsibility is the *willingness and ability to honor our promises and commitments even when this involves hardship.* Responsible people will endure sacrifice to keep their word. And because their given word means a lot to them, they do not make promises quickly or carelessly.

- Responsibility is the *habit of minding our own business, staying out of matters that do not concern us.* Mature people do not snoop, gossip, or meddle. They consistently give people the benefit of the doubt and they respect people's right to the presumption of innocence. Savvy bosses know that gossips tend to be slackers; those employees who meddle in everyone else's business usually neglect their own.

Here's an important lesson for your future as a family man: Responsible children learn from their parents' example how to use their powers to contribute to family welfare. They receive encouragement as well as correction from their parents, and so they grow in confidence. In a real sense, *responsibility is another word for maturity*. Children do not become mature when they reach puberty and grow in physical stature, but when they think and act consistently like other-centered adults.

You can explain it this way to your youngsters later. Responsibility means just this: If we don't do what we're supposed to do, somebody else gets hurt. We do our duty so that other people won't suffer. That's why responsibility is another word for love.

Fortitude

Fortitude is the third great virtue. We also know it by other names: *courage, perseverance, toughness, "guts."*

Outside of war or some physical threat to our safety (as in our poorest city neighborhoods), physical courage isn't often needed in civilized society. But moral courage certainly is. Living a moral life means taking risks and grappling with hardship—including the problem of looking different from our peers. Many adults never learned this concept while growing up, never knew firsthand any sort of adversity. For this, they and their families suffer.

Here are some ways of looking at this power:

- Fortitude is the *acquired ability either to overcome or endure difficulties: pain, discomfort, disappointment, setbacks, worry, tedium, looking "different."* It is the strength of will either to solve a given problem or just live with it—but in no case to seek irresponsible escape.

  How many dreadful problems among teens and young married couples spring from a fixed, habitual resort to escape—that is, from young people's low tolerance for hardship or even inconvenience? How is this weakness related to our problems with drugs and alcohol abuse and so much of our staggering divorce rate?

- *Personal toughness is a habit of overcoming anxiety through purposeful, honorable action.* We turn our worries into action. It is the opposite of whining inertia in the face of problems, a compulsion to feckless complaint. Courageous people, in fact, see escapism—fleeing from inconvenience—as unworthy, even dishonorable.

  Personal courage, enhanced by sound judgment, means coming to terms with a fact of reality: life brings hardships, and many of these are unavoidable, even insoluble. But we adults learn to cope with them as best we can; we just put them behind us and get on with life. Related to this is the realistic understanding that, most of the time, expectation hurts more than reality: problems nearly always seem worse in advance than they turn out to be once we tackle them.

- To look at it another way, this strength of fortitude is a *confidence in our problem-solving abilities, built through a lifetime practice of solving problems.* Athletics, jobs around the house, schoolwork and homework, meeting deadlines, working at our best under reasonable pressure—all these build courage and self-confidence. So does steady, affirming encouragement from parents and sometimes good bosses: "You can do it if you try." "Stick with it and you can lick it." "You're stronger than you think."

When or if you are someday a father, please remember this. Some reasonable adversity is healthy for children. There's such a thing as good stress. Outside of certain misguided schools, nobody in society "works at his own pace." If our forebears had worked at their own pace, we would still be riding in donkey carts and lighting our homes with candles. It took gutsy risk-taking and sustained hard work to produce our wondrous labor-saving devices. When we're under reasonable stress, we all do our best work.

- Fortitude is also the *determination to overcome personal shortcomings.* This means making the most of the good side of our natural temperament while working to overcome the downside. If we are shy, we learn to be a friendly, attentive listener, for a "good listener" usually attracts good friends. If we're impulsive, we learn to restrain ourselves from excess and foresee consequences; we direct our zestful energy to achievement. If we are lazy, we strive toward purposeful action. If we fail to understand something, we seek advice from people we respect and otherwise think matters through. And so on.

In a real sense, the power of fortitude is the exact

opposite of "getting in touch with our feelings," a woefully common outlook today. To be sure, sentiment has its place in life. Powerful emotions of love and loyalty, directed as they are to others' welfare, can move us to greatness. But in real life, self-centered feelings must give way to duty; if they do not, then people have practically no capacity for *sacrifice*, which is the absolute essence of real love. Genuine love means *ignoring our self-centered feelings for the sake of others*. In grown-up life, love means serving others courageously. To be a great parent takes guts.

Self-mastery

The fourth great virtue, *self-mastery* or temperance, is one of the virtues we esteem most in people. In our self-indulgent culture, a temperate man or woman stands out from the crowd. Sometimes, especially in one's teens and twenties, it takes courage to resist peer pressures and stand apart as one's own master.

Children grab for pleasures and power. They give free rein to their appetites and passions and doggedly resist the word "no." In a sense, they're often enslaved to their fears and feelings. If they grow up this way, they are headed for serious trouble.

No question about it, there's a lot riding on how well or badly parents lead their children to control themselves, and curb their children's passions and cravings by artful use of the word "no." What does self-mastery mean? What should you teach your children about it, and its urgent importance?

- Temperance is the power to say *no*, at will, to our laziness, passions, and appetites. It is the power, built up through practice, to *wait* for rewards, and to *earn* them. A self-controlled man or woman, like everyone else, wants instant gratification but does not expect it or need it. Self-controlled people do not turn wants into needs, and they know the difference.

- Self-indulgent people grab for gratifications now and put off hard effort for later. Self-controlled people do just the opposite. They have a lifetime habit of earning what they want.

- Temperance means *sensible enjoyment.* Self-controlled people enjoy the pleasures of life in moderation, never (or hardly ever) to excess. They don't go overboard in food, drink, entertainment, or even work. Because they are self-directed, they appear to others as quietly self-confident, on top of life. Their enjoyment comes from other people, not just things.

- Temperance means *mastery of one's speech and actions.* Self-controlled people do not use coarse language gratuitously. Only some rare, outrageous provocation prods them to cussing, and they follow up with apologies when called for. They have a habit of controlling their speech and thereby showing respect for the people around them.

- Temperance means *mastery of one's time and affairs.* Self-controlled people know how to manage time. In fact, the business catchword "time management" is just another name for self-control. Self-disciplined people know how to plan ahead, set their own deadlines, and stick to them. They neither exaggerate nor underestimate the size of a task and the time needed to complete it.

- Temperance means *habitual courtesy.* Self-disciplined people have a lifelong habit of saying and meaning *please, thank you, I'm sorry,* and *I give my word. . . .* If they offend anyone, even unintentionally, they are quick to apologize. They extend courtesy to everyone, and they can do this even in the face of rudeness or provocation.

In a word, temperate people have "class." Their character is marked by self-restraint, etiquette, healthy self-respect, an active spirit of service and an ongoing and active concern for the dignity and needs of those around them. To everyone who knows them, they are esteemed as great friends.

Heart

Last of all, *greatness of heart.* This is the all-important spiritual power that gives force to all the other virtues. It directs our powers of judgment, responsibility, toughness, and self-control toward the well-being of other people, starting with our family and radiating out to friends, colleagues, acquaintances, strangers, and our country.

The ancient Romans called it *magnanimity,* "greatness of soul." In our Judeo-Christian tradition, it goes by other names: *charity, compassionate understanding, awareness of others' needs, a spirit of service, sacrificial love.*

It is the capacity and desire to surpass ourselves, to endure or overcome anything for the sake of somebody else's welfare and happiness. It is *generosity*—the drive to give others the best of what we have for their sake and expect little or nothing in return.

Where does someone put his heart? What does he love most in life? What would he be willing to suffer for and even die for? Answer these questions, and you put your finger on that person's values.

The fact is, everyone has values. Everyone holds something closest to his heart and leaves other things at a distance.

To speak of people's values, therefore, is to speak of their *priorities* in life: what comes first with them, then what comes second, third, and on down the line. Where, in what order, do people put their passions? What do they love most?

People differ in their values because they differ in what they love most and least. Look at this list of things that people love and live for—what they passionately pursue as the object of their heart:

- God
- family and friends
- country
- money
- truth
- fame and glory
- satisfying, service-oriented work
- career advancement
- comfort and convenience
- addictive substances

- pleasure and amusement
- power over others
- safety and security
- conformity: acceptance by others, being fashionably "with it"
- vengeance

We can tell people's values by which of these loves they hold closest, and which they belittle or ignore.

Up to now, we've been studying, among other things, what children must learn in order to become mature adults. But here, in the question of heart, we look at what adults must learn from children. As you grow into an adult, keep this in mind.

In the third century B.C., the Chinese philosopher Mencius said, "A great person is one who never loses the heart he had as a child."

It's obvious (once we see it) that the great character strengths have to be formed from scratch in children as they grow up, for kids do not enter the world with judgment, responsibility, courage, or self-control. But children do nonetheless have beautiful qualities that must survive intact throughout childhood and into later life.

It's true, parents must patiently lead their children to become adults who are competent, learned, tough-minded, responsible, shrewd and savvy, nobody's fool. But at the same time, as they grow up, children should never lose the great loves that they had as small children, loves they see still alive and growing in you.

What are these great loves of childhood? What do you strive to live by . . . so you can someday teach your children?

- *Love for God.* Once they've been taught religious faith by their parents, children have a humble, sincere, and beautiful trust in God, whom they see as an all-powerful, all-loving Father.

  As adults, great people never lose this vision and faith of childhood. They see themselves as children of God all their lives, watched over by the Creator's loving protection. This hope-filled confidence empowers them to withstand any hardship in life and steels them with a stalwart sense of responsibility, ethical uprightness, a clean conscience, what the Scriptures call "righteousness." God lives in the home, not just in church.

- *Love for family.* Tiny children have a natural and abiding affection for parents and brothers and sisters, who are the compass of their young hearts, the center of their existence.

  All their lives, adults should hold onto their loving trust in Dad and Mom, loyalty to their grown brothers and sisters, and wholehearted devotion to the families they form themselves. As in childhood, their families form the center of their lives.

- *Love for life, friends, laughter.* Children arise each morning seeing the day as an adventure, a call to delight and achievement with family and friends. With their loved ones they share the gift of laughter, that splendid sign of a light, clean heart.

  So, too, as adults they should be moved by that same vision of life as an adventure, enjoying each day as a gift, delighting in the companionship of friends.

They should take their responsibilities seriously, but not themselves.

- *Love for those in need.* At their best, youngsters have an exquisite quality of mercy, a capacity for compassion. We see this in their tender care for a wounded little animal, or their heartfelt sympathy for a grieving friend. This capacity for mercy, feeling sorry for someone, must never be snuffed out.

  All their lives, great men and women show mercy to others, extending their hearts and help to people in trouble. They "hate sin but love the sinner." They strive for peace, forgive injuries, bear no ill will or grudges toward anyone. They know that charity does not mean donating old clothes; it means mostly compassionate understanding.

- *Love for the truth.* Tiny children, it seems, are naturally truthful; they are laughably inept when they first try to lie. They have a way of putting their little fingers right on the truth, often with startling insight, like the candid little boy in *The Emperor's New Clothes.* Instinctively and with astonishing accuracy, they can judge people's character.

  So also in adulthood, they should shun all forms of phoniness. They should have the guts to tell the truth, admit when they're wrong, and apologize. They should never enslave themselves to the worst lie of all: self-deception. They should know who they are and what they stand for: lessons learned from Dad and Mom.

Great people, then, are those who possess within their souls the powers of adults and the hearts of children. Generously, they direct their lives to the needs of others, and they have the inner strengths to serve people effectively, starting with their families. To all who know them, they are "wise as serpents and innocent as doves" (Mt 10:16)—great men and women.

All this is an ideal for your life as a man, and the lives of those whom God will put in your care.

CHAPTER 3

Getting Along with People

Getting along well with people is the key to almost every success in family life and business and professional affairs. It's absolutely crucial to the strength and soundness of your judgment.

If you were to ask older experienced professionals and family men (as I have) what advice they'd give about dealing with people honorably and shrewdly, what sort of insights would they provide? Here are some that I've picked up from various sources. Please think carefully about each one.

- You can tell a lot about people's quality by . . .

  —the kind of friends they choose

  —the heroes they admire

  —the vigor and joy that they put into their work

  —how they treat their parents and siblings

  —the measure of affectionate respect they earn from their children

  —how kind they are to other people's children

  —how they treat people over them and under them at work

  —whether they're friendly toward everyone or just to people they can use

  —how competently and considerately they drive a car

—what they laugh at

—what they most often talk about; what is closest to their hearts.

- Everybody is a package deal, a mixture of good qualities and shortcomings. If you look for defects in people, you'll always find them. People who habitually harp on people's faults are really, deep down, unhappy with themselves.

- When people complain too much about some fault in others, they're unwittingly revealing their own dominant flaw. For instance—inert people are annoyed by others' laziness. Inconsiderate people are irked by perceived rudeness. Disorganized people can't stand others' messes. People who are casual about the truth are quick to assume that others are lying. Phonies see hypocrisy all around them. Gossips fear betrayal of their confidence. Control freaks gripe about "tyranny."

- The whole world, it seems, is divided into two types of people. On one side are the vast majority: normal, decent people who seek goodness, truth, and beauty in life. They find these delights in family, friendship, work, leisure, sports, art, nature, and other healthy human interests. On the other side are the minority: those who single-mindedly grasp after *power*. They devote themselves to imposing their will by bullying or manipulating others. They value people only for their usefulness; they treat words as weapons; they break promises when it suits them; they lust for gossip and traffic in it; they promote their interests above anyone else's rights; they're preoccupied, even obsessed, with the architectonics of control. Avoid these people. Try not to work under them. Above all, if possible, don't vote them into public office.

- The happiest people are those who can forget their self-interests and direct their powers toward the welfare of others.

- We do not really forgive unless we also forget. To dwell on past grievances is evil and destructive. Similarly, to refuse someone's sincere apology is dishonorable.

- A life given over to sensual pleasure is relentlessly greedy, never satisfied, and ultimately lonely. But a life devoted to spirit—turned to God, goodness, truth, beauty—brings happiness and peace of mind.

- People "in touch with their feelings" seldom amount to much. Real achievement nearly always requires *overcoming* our feelings.

- Immature people do not distinguish between wants and needs. They're also ingrates. They care for neither their own parents nor their children, if they have any.

- An ideology is the lust for power disguised as a noble ideal.

- Good friendships bring out the best in us.

- Real friendship is based on mutual respect, not just warm feelings. The deepest, most long-lasting friendships arise among people who greatly respect each other's character.

- A real friend is someone you don't have to pretend with, and couldn't even if you wanted to. A real friend will take risks for you. A real friend extends you understanding, sympathy, and time.

- Apart from our family and religious principles, close friends are our greatest help in making important decisions.

- One sign of deep friendship: You and your friend can share silence together, as when you drive somewhere sitting side by side. Silences aren't awkward. Only superficial acquaintances feel a need to fill time with chatter.

- Beware of so-called friends who offer to lie for you in order to get you out of trouble. If they'd lie *for* you, they'd also lie *to* you. People are never dishonest in just one part of their lives.

- Cynics are people who habitually mistrust the honesty and good intentions of others. Very often they do this to justify their own nastiness. That is, they project onto others the mean spirit inside themselves. Sometimes people will affect a cynical attitude because they think it implies wide experience in life, something which they lack. That's why if you scratch a cynic, you'll usually find an insecure naïf.

- Don't give advice unless you're asked for it, and then keep it brief. Remember, too, that when people seek advice from you, what they really want is encouragement.

- The opposite of love is not hatred, but indifference. In some ways, indifference is more painful than hatred. When we're indifferent to people, we treat them as though they were mere objects, things of no consequence. Hatred points accusingly at behavior, but indifference directly attacks one's dignity as a person.

- Confident, considerate people are never afraid to

apologize. When you have a quarrel with someone (especially your wife), be the first to say, "I'm sorry; please forgive me."

- If anyone is offended by something you said or did, say you're sorry even if you didn't mean to give offense. You can always honestly say, "I'm sorry your feelings were hurt."

- Good manners are the way we show respect for other people's rights and dignity. Because courtesy shows good judgment and self-control, it wins people's respect. When we show respect to others, we usually gain their respect in turn.

- "Thank you" is always an appropriate response to any kind of praise or favor. When you're at a loss for words to respond, say "thank you" and let it go at that.

- When you want to praise someone, make it sincere and brief. If you overdo praise, it sounds phony.

- Never fail to send a thank-you note immediately for gifts, job interviews, and substantial favors.

- Tedium is part of life. Most really important accomplishments in life—moving up in a career, forming a stable family life, mastering some skill—involve stretches of repetitive and apparently nonproductive action. Having a great goal or ideal is what turns drudgery into an adventurous and sporting pursuit.

- When good-willed people are angry with each other, the main causes are threefold: (a) misunderstanding caused by miscommunication, (b) tight deadlines and other extraneous pressures, or (c) sheer physical fatigue. Under these circumstances, even good-natured people can lose control of their tempers. Remember this when you are married. Be patient with your loved ones and never let the sun go down on your anger. The first to apologize is the winner.

- Our moral principles are our compass in life, and they simplify life's choices. To people without principles, life is always complicated.

- We should always maintain an open mind, but not so open that our brains fall out.

- Fear in the face of adversity is nothing to be ashamed of. In fact, it's a sign of intelligence, for only fools are never afraid. Courage consists of doing our duty in spite of our fears. Do we handle the problem as best we can, relying on God's help . . . or do we just run away?

- Self-pity is, at best, a waste of time and psychic energy. It causes "yesterday" to crowd out too much of "today."

- Money is just an instrument for the welfare of our loved ones and those in need. And that's all it is.

- Responsibility is unavoidable in life, for we all answer to somebody—family, bosses, clients, customers, the law. Everybody answers to God.

- Deep down, people's greatest need is to feel appreciated. This is true in family life, friendship, and the workplace.

- If you walk tall and smile a lot, you'll look years younger.

- For those who truly and deeply love God, life becomes a grand and comic sporting adventure.

- The real riches in life are family, friends, faith, and a clear conscience. Everything else is gravy.

CHAPTER 4

University Life

If you are still a college or university student, you may find the points in this chapter useful. As with other matters in this book, you may or may not agree with everything that's said, but at least the ideas will prompt you to think. Everything here has taken shape over several years in my conversations with university students and professors.

If you've finished your post-secondary schooling, you might want to pass on these insights and pieces of advice to young people you know. What follows here, rounded off with your experience, may be a great service to your younger friends.

In any event, see how much of the following you agree with and perhaps wish you'd learned earlier.

Some Approaches to Study

- You are enrolled in an educational institution in order to grow, not just in skills and information, but in strengths of character—to acquire habits of sound judgment, a sense of responsibility, personal toughness (perseverance), and self-mastery (the ability to say *no* to yourself). You are really out to improve your professional/personal powers of *concentration of mind and will* and *getting along well with people.*

- Study, like any other serious undertaking, requires

planning, effort, and continual reflective improvement (quality control). This is not a "hassle" but an investment. Success in study is mostly a matter of attitude and acquired habits, not intelligence.

- Plan to work an eight-hour or nine-hour day, which is normal in the professional world.

- Time is a resource, and the purpose of planning is to *have more time*. People who plan effectively manage to create more time as well as gain more control over themselves and their environment. To plan effectively, you need to . . .

  —gather information first: keep a time log, and note where time's misused now

  —look ahead: use a calendar to foresee deadlines and set your own targets

  —take in the big picture: recognize how present studies lead to long-term professional goals

- Remember the 80/20 rule—80 percent of successful results come from 20 percent of work. So, you should work from priorities. The first 20 percent of your study time is the hardest; once you've started well, the rest proceeds with efficient momentum. Also note that some courses are more important than others; these should receive your top attention.

- Give top priority, greatest concentration, to courses that are (a) cumulative, such as mathematics, certain sciences, and languages, (b) necessary to long-term professional goals, such as sciences or history.

- Work to establish a routine without being enslaved

by it. Successful professionals strike a balance between scheduled routine and flexibility. Have set times to *begin* work, concentrating on top-priority tasks. Use odds and ends of time (e.g., riding the bus, waiting for rides) to do "grunt" tasks: reviewing vocabulary from flashcards, "questioning" notes from class (i.e., noting where you want or need to ask questions of your instructor), planning a sequence of studies for the evening.

- Pay attention to your biorhythms. If you're sluggish right after dinner but perk up an hour later, then do lower priority work right after eating and save higher priority work for hours when you're more alert. If sugar seems to tire you, don't eat a heavy carbohydrate breakfast or lunch, especially if your first two classes thereafter are high priority.

- One difference from high-school work is reliance on team study. Certainly you will learn a lot by studying alone, but you can reinforce your learning by meeting with classmates and exchanging ideas, swapping questions, and otherwise preparing for exams together. Research among universities shows that this team-study approach is highly effective for learning in depth and improving academic performance.

- Here's something very important to grasp at the outset: One of the character strengths you must cultivate in college is *self-control* (i.e., the virtues of fortitude and temperance). You need to become what you must be all your life: a self-starter, a person of initiative and healthy balance, a person who foresees consequences and directs personal affairs with sound judgment. It's very important in college to manage your time and treat it as a resource, so that you control events and don't let events control you. This means, among other things, going to bed and getting up on time, working from a sensible plan, saying "no" to temptations to slack off or otherwise indulge your sloth or appetites. Remember, the term "time management" is just another term for "self-control." Regardless of the talents or skills you have, if you don't acquire habits of self-control at this age, you'll never amount to anything. This may sound strong, but it's the truth.

- Study to learn, to strengthen your judgment, not just to do well on tests. You will eventually forget most of the "material"—and an education is what you have left over after you've forgotten it. What really counts is what happens inside your mind, will, and heart. Your whole educational experience should lead you to grow in several important areas: strength of discerning judgment, understanding of history and present events, insight into people, the ability to concentrate, the ability to control your affairs (self-mastery), the ability to make distinctions and solve problems persistently, the ability to get along with people of different backgrounds and personalities, and the power to take responsibility for the professional quality of your work.

Dealing with people

- The college experience is essentially that of cultivating excellent ideas and people—quality books and quality friends. Its aim is to enhance your growth in cordial familiarity with the finest achievements of the human spirit—and to find and befriend people who share your principle values, people who might become friends for life.

- Some advice for getting along well with people and forming habits that will enhance your later career:

  —Don't eat alone. Find someone who is eating alone and ask to join him or her at the table. Practice meeting people and making new friends.

  —Don't complain about how overworked you are; everybody's busy and no one wants to be bored by your whining.

  —Mind your own business. Don't say negative things about people behind their backs. Nobody likes or trusts a gossip.

  —Don't make promises lightly; for if you do promise something, you're obligated to keep your word.

  —Be generous in thanking people; make the words "thank you" a frequent part of your speech. Remember that a person's greatest need is to be genuinely appreciated.

- Work to stay in good physical shape with habits of physical exercise, adequate sleep, and sensible nutrition. If you get into good shape by the time you're twenty, you'll probably stay that way for many years.

- Get to know your professors and get them to know you—and to respect you for your competence, character, drive, and honorable ambition. In a few years, some of them can and will write recommendations important for your career. They can only do this if they know and respect you.

- Learn to write clearly and convincingly. Listen to your professors' comments about your writing and take their advice seriously. Pretend that every essay of yours is a letter, something you're writing to a friend who's interested in your thinking. This approach to writing makes it easier to get started, easy to continue, and much more interesting. Always read your work aloud to yourself before submitting it; goofs are more easily spotted this way. Use your university years to find out where your writing needs improvement. Don't wait until your first job to learn this; it could hurt your career and therefore your ability to support your family.

- A philosopher once defined education this way: "Choose your company carefully, and then listen." When it comes time to choose elective courses (especially in history, philosophy, and literature), choose on the basis of the *professor*, not course content. Ask around to find out who are the very best teachers and then sign up for their courses. The best teachers will challenge you intellectually and personally, and their courses will probably be interesting. (That's interesting, not entertaining—and you should know the difference.) Moreover, their courses might open up new avenues toward a career. Many professionals first launched their careers by studying under excellent, inspiring teachers.

- Be true to your principles—those moral and religious values you learned from your parents and other principled adults whom you respected in high school. When you meet with ideas that conflict with your principles, you should spot them for what they are and set them aside. Remember what an Oxford don once said: "The purpose of education is that young people should know rubbish when they see it." Cultivate a healthy skepticism. As another teacher put it, "Always maintain an open mind, but not so open that your brains fall out."

- Choose your roommates carefully. If possible, share your space with people who share your principles and sense of decorum but who are different enough (in tastes, interests, background) to be interesting. If the housing office pairs you with someone uncivilized, do whatever's necessary to make a change. You need peace of mind to study, and this is hard to achieve when you share living space with a primitive.

- When dealing with personnel in university offices, be both friendly and assertive. If you have a problem (say, with changing roommates or courses), don't take "no" for an answer, but be nice about it. A good-natured but determined persistence generally gets you very far with college officials. Be especially nice to administrative staff. In universities as in the business world, the secretaries make things happen. They run the country.

- Regardless of your major, use your college years to

master at least one foreign language. College graduates consistently rate mastery of a language as one of their most rewarding experiences.

- Also regardless of your major, take at least one course in art or music appreciation and study of a foreign literature in translation, including classical literature. Russian literature is especially rich in moral meaning, for the Russians addressed the great questions in life. These studies may be the beginning of lifetime cultural enjoyment, no matter what you do later for a living.

- Pace yourself so that you work a forty-five hour week, which is normal in professional life. Count on averaging eight hours a day of classes and study, occasionally more as necessary. If you press yourself to work in scheduled blocks of hours, you'll make time for recreation and friendship. Don't live the way many immature college students do, with drudgery during the week and debauchery on weekends. People like this enjoy neither work nor play, and they run themselves into the ground.

- As for your partying and social life (a normal part of the college experience), remember what St. Don Bosco used to tell his young friends: "Always remain in the state of grace . . . and enjoy life as much as you can!" God wants us to enjoy the good gifts he sends us in normal life—food, drink, friendship, play, work—but never to the point of offending him.

- Related to this, remember that beer is not a soft drink with a buzz. It's an alcoholic drink, to be used sensibly and temperately. Alcohol is a drug, drunkenness is a grave sin, and intemperance often leads to other grave sins and tragedies—crippling or fatal accidents, pregnancies, abortions, or a desperate struggle with alcoholism. Every year these scourges afflict many university students, even well-intentioned young people from good homes. These are youths who, unfortunately grew up with every advantage except the ones that count most: sound judgment, Christian conscience, and the power of self-control.

CHAPTER 5

Cultural Formation

Set out on purpose to become a "lifelong learner." No matter what field you work in, a pursuit of cultural enjoyment should be part of your life. If you deepen your familiarity with the finest achievements of the human spirit, you will strengthen your judgment about people and events, enjoy life more fully, give good example to your children, and earn the respect of everyone who knows you.

So how does a busy man go about using his time well to deepen his cultural formation? Here are some approaches to keep in mind from the experiences of others:

- Treat reading and cultural experiences (listening to music, visiting museums, and the like) as a new hobby, almost like taking up a new sport. Many men who never formed a habit of reading, or who had only a technical education (in, say, engineering or business), began to read history, biography, and literature when in their thirties, forties, or even later—and found a new source of enjoyment in life. They found this new direction to be relaxing, enjoyable, and invigorating, just like any other hobby. The more they got into it, the more enjoyable it became.

- Depend on recommendations. Ask people whose judgment you respect for suggestions. Seeking and following sound advice is one way to use time well.

- Start with biographies and narrative histories, even military history. Most adult males find these genres interesting and attractive, generally more so (at least initially) than literature. Many men lament that no one ever introduced them to biography and narrative history when they were in school because most "outside reading" was confined to fictional works, many of them mediocre at best. Fact: About 80 percent of readers who belong to the History Book Club are men. (This organization, similar to the Book-of-the Month Club, is worth looking into.)

- Take your time. A good book is worth reading fairly slowly, cover to cover. You'll probably be surprised how much you can read in short takes. If you read about a page a minute, and read only twenty minutes a day, you can read about one book a month, twelve books a year. If you "read" high-quality audio books in your car, you can accomplish even more. For busy, culture-seeking men, the car's audio equipment is one of the best inventions of our era—an excellent way to make good use of time.

- Consider concentrating on one great author and read several of his or her works: Dickens, Dostoyevsky, Tolstoy, Shakespeare, Conrad, Flannery O'Connor, and so on. The Russians are especially rich in probing the great moral questions. Don't let it put you off if you read some of these authors in high school and were bored by them. The great works were written for mature adults, people experienced in living. It's a pity that young people often lose interest in great literature simply because of a premature exposure.

- To look at the issue another way: Get rid of books that contribute nothing to your judgment. You wouldn't eat trash. Why put it in your head?

- Some people find it helpful to start by making a log for a week or two of where time normally goes during the day. Most are surprised to see how much goes into fluff like indiscriminate television-watching or surfing the Net. These blocks of time are a good place to begin your program of reading, and thereby give good example to your children.

- If possible, try reading, or at least skimming, the same books your children are reading in school. Help them see your own experienced, adult point of view. Query them about what you are both reading together. Take an interest—on purpose—in what their minds are up to.

- Visit art museums with your friends and children. If one or two artists catch your eye, read up on their life and other works. Aside from that, read a couple of books on composition in painting; most men, especially the technically oriented, find this approach to art very engaging. It enhances their appreciation for artistic accomplishment.

- Take an interest in some classical music. Start with one or two composers, such as Beethoven or Mozart. Here too, once they get into it and understand what's going on, most adult males find some classical music very appealing and enjoyable. Listening to favorite works, at home or in the car, becomes a lifelong way to relax.

- Last of all, see the time you put into cultural formation as an *investment*. Like taking up a new sport (golf, for instance), the experience may be a bit awkward at first but becomes progressively more enjoyable.

CHAPTER 6

An Overview of Professionalism

Want a short definition of professionalism? Here's one: Professionalism is the virtues as they're lived and shown in the workplace. Prudence, justice, fortitude, self-control, faith, hope, and charity—these qualities affect the way we work and give strength to our character. Below are some ways of understanding the very important concept of professionalism. Think about each of them. Have you seen examples of what's described below?

- Professionalism isn't just a set of appearances—neatness, good grooming, "shoptalk," and the like. Nor is it just technical skill, for many technically skilled people are not really professional. Professionalism is, rather, a set of internalized character strengths and values directed toward high quality service to others through one's work. In their daily work, real professionals show these inner strengths and attitudes—sound judgment, know-how, business savvy, mature responsibility, problem-solving perseverance and ingenuity, along with what people call "class." This is as true for hairdressers, carpenters, machinists, police officers, and barbers as it is for lawyers, physicians, and engineers. Any honest work can be done professionally.

- Professionals show self-respect in their work. They're conscious that work reflects their inner character.

Their work is, among other things, a statement of their personal commitment to excellence of performance. They don't see work as just a job to be done or merely a source of "spending money."

- Professionals see work as service to others. They labor for the betterment of other people, directly or indirectly: clients, customers, employers, colleagues. Thus they're both *task-oriented* and *people-oriented.*

- Professionals have respect for experience. They have an ongoing need to learn and improve, to master traditional approaches and *then* try to improve on them. That's why there's a teaching tradition among professionals; people teach and learn by word and example. Professionals also respect the experience of others; they have high regard for professionalism in other lines of work. Moreover, they know how to use the powers of other professionals (lawyers, accountants, consultants) to strengthen their own performance. They seek out sound advice and generally follow it.

- Professionals tend to see problems as challenges and opportunities, not burdensome "hassles" to be avoided. They have a long-term habit of approaching problems confidently and optimistically. They don't let indecision or fear of failure cause paralysis. They do the best they can with what they have.

- Professionals have a high level of personal responsibility and respect for others' rights. They have a clear sense of the *limits* to their authority and rights of operation. They don't meddle in others' affairs or criticize in areas where they have neither rights nor expertise. Professionals are unafraid to say, "That's none of my business" or "I don't know anything about that. . . ." They tend to have an intense dislike for gossip or otherwise uninformed criticism.

- Professionals make efficient use of resources, especially time. They know how to concentrate their mind and will on the tasks before them. They work quickly but not hurriedly. They're careful but not slow.

- Professionals compartmentalize work responsibilities from leisure and personal interests. Work hours are devoted exclusively to the job; leisure and personal affairs wait until the job is done. Responsibilities to clients and employers come ahead of self-interested concerns and pleasures. They know that leisure is most enjoyable when it's been earned through hard work. They can do their best work no matter how poorly they feel at the moment.

- Even off the job, professionals generally show admirable character: good judgment, good taste, good manners, a respect for quality in general. Their personality shows tasteful self-restraint combined with concern for others and love of life—in a word, "class."

- The character and values of professionalism are built up first in childhood and then strengthened in adulthood through study, training, and work experience. This means that young people, including teenagers, can mark themselves as professionals—earn the respect of all who work with them—during the first few weeks of their first job.

CHAPTER 7

Pursuing a Successful Career

Finding what you're good at and using this knowledge to pursue a career are common concerns—not to say serious worries—among young people aged eighteen to twenty-five.

How can a young man go about finding and pursuing his professional vocation? What should be his approach and attitude? What is the best advice from people with expertise in this area? Here are some key ideas and practical approaches.

- Success in a career doesn't necessarily mean great fame and big money. Real success in work and life means several other things:
    —living with a clean conscience before God
    —being able to support yourself and your family comfortably
    —waking up in the morning and looking forward to the day's work
    —earning the respect of everyone who knows you
    —seeing your powers and skills operate for the betterment of others
    —enjoying leisure pursuits thoroughly because you've *earned* them.

- There's such a thing as a professional vocation. It's some passionate love that directs your powers to the welfare of others and earns you a living. You should search long and wide to find a line of work that appeals to your heart—some labor that gives you the joy you knew in childhood, when work and play were one. Few pleasures in life are more delightful than a job we really enjoy.

- One word of caution, though. You may love music or drama or sports so much that you think of these fields as potential careers. Fine, but anchor yourself in reality. Entertainment and sports bring delight to millions. Hundreds of thousands of young people aspire to work in these fields—and everyone in this vast throng is competing against you. To succeed, you must be exceptionally talented, extremely hardworking, single-mindedly ambitious, well connected with influential people, and (to be frank about it) very, very lucky. The odds are hugely against you. Remember, no matter what you later do for a living, you can always enjoy these pursuits as recreational pastimes.

- Anyone seeking a career should take this advice: look hard and *keep* looking. Be alert to meeting people, hearing about opportunities, asking around, networking with everyone you know. Have the mentality of a taxi driver cruising around on the lookout for business. The world's inventions and discoveries (like Goodyear's vulcanized rubber or Edison's electric bulb) were achieved by people who were *looking* for something.

- Some professionals advise young people to get a job, any job, and use that as a basis for moving ahead. A job that puts you in touch with a lot of people, such as sales, seems to work best. What you learn on the job, especially if you have a good boss, can help you a lot to bring what you want into clearer focus and then make a career move.

- Rely on family and friends to tell you what you're really good at. Often someone who is good at something is among the last to know it. Others notice our talent before we do. Why? Because to us the gift seems natural, easy, almost effortless. Pay attention when people close to you all say you have a gift that you should develop.

- Throughout history, finding a good career and a good job has always been a matter of whom you know. Credentials, experience, cold calls, mass mailings of résumés—none of these things beat *connections through friends.* Most likely your friends won't have a job for you, but *their* friends might. We get a job most quickly and effectively through the friends of our friends. For this reason—among many others, of course—it pays to have many friends and acquaintances. (Related piece of advice: Strive to stay in contact with your closest friends from high school and college. Work at making them friends for life.)

- Know the difference between a referral and a reference. A referral is just an introduction: someone you know socially introduces you to a friend or acquaintance who might be interested in hiring you. This is basically vouching for your character, without comment or judgment about your technical competence, something your friend may not be in a position to know. A reference, on the other hand, is an assessment of both your character and your professional competence based on that person's knowledge about your work.

- Before you use anyone's name as a reference, be sure to get that person's permission. Prospective employers nearly always check references, so failure to secure prior permission from someone makes your reference worse than useless. You may mark yourself as immature, amateurish, or inconsiderate.

- Your mother had the right idea: Say "thank you" frequently. People like to be appreciated. Moreover, in this way you mark yourself as mature and pleasant to deal with. Related to this, keep good quality stationery on hand to send thank-you notes for favors.

- Every few months, take a couple of hours to think deeply about your career and your future. *How are things going? Where am I headed? What opportunities might I be overlooking? Where do I want to be five years down the road?* Have a file where you keep notes on accomplishments to update your résumé, and do this at least twice a year. An updated résumé is like a first-aid kit: if you need it at all, you need it in a hurry.

- As you move along Plan A of your career, maintain a Plan B as well—an alternative career course to rely on if you suddenly must. If someone loses a job, he or she quickly needs to undertake thinking, planning, networking, and action. Maintaining a Plan B means doing your thinking, planning, and networking ahead of time, long before the emergency, so you can move swiftly into action. Be prepared for anything.

- Always remember that the secret of success is passion, so think big. We tend to become what we think about. If you have high ambitions of *service* to people, starting with your family, you'll be honored as an outstanding man and an excellent professional.

CHAPTER 8

Collaborating with Bosses

A huge part of young people's success in their professional career derives from their collaboration with bosses. Here are some words of advice for young people on how to collaborate with business leaders and learn from them.

- In your first couple of jobs, try to work for a good boss, someone who'll challenge your powers, correct you, and help you learn from your mistakes. A good boss will teach you more things of a practical nature in one year than you'll learn in four years of college.

- Notice that successful bosses have effective communication skills: they're attentive listeners and clear explainers. They learn from people, including their employees. They lead their people to understand what's important. They help their people form the same picture, especially of where everyone is headed and how each person's effort contributes to reaching that goal. Learn from your boss how to deal effectively with people, how to be a leader. (Notice that an effective leader has *joiners*, not followers; he or she takes action toward some goal and persuades others to collaborate in the venture. Moreover, his or her exercise of authority is really a form of service.)

- The boss is your key customer. Your aim is to keep your boss pleased with your work and pleased with you as a person. One of the fundamental facts in business is that bosses tend to hire and retain competent people whom they personally like and respect—people of integrity, hard work, and good humor.

- Work in such a way that you make your boss look good.

- Keep your boss in the loop. No surprises. Bosses generally hate surprises.

- Ask for a raise when you think you've earned it.

- Don't take problems to your boss without also proposing some considered solutions. Bosses don't need additional problems; they have enough as it is. What they need and want are solutions.

- When your boss gives you a project, reach an understanding with him or her right away about how much time it should take. Try to deliver it ahead of time and to the best of your ability.

- Personal integrity is crucially important in business. Tell nothing but the truth and always keep your word. Bosses and clients can forgive isolated, well-intentioned mistakes and even blunders—but if you lie, you're through.

- What are the faults that can get you fired?

  —Lying on your résumé (calls for instant dismissal).

  —Being difficult to work with, having trouble getting along with others.

  —Failing to treat others with respect.

  —Spreading rumors or not maintaining confidentiality.

—Not paying attention to detail.

—Not following through on commitments.

- Unless you're the boss, it's not your job to change company policies. If you find policies or ongoing practices very hard to live with, don't complain. Just look for another job and try to leave on good terms. During your next job interview, or when you get another job, don't bad-mouth your previous company or its management. Remember, bosses tend to sympathize with each other as a class. Your perceived disloyalty to former employers will leave a bad taste and arouse mistrust.

CHAPTER 9

Professional and Business Savvy

As we all know, talents and skills are important to success in professional life. But other personal qualities are also extremely important. These are the details of etiquette, honest and honorable dealings with others, and level-headed shrewdness that are expressed in the word *savvy*. Normally these details are not taught in school. They are passed down mostly from one's parents and older friends. We include some here, all based on people's professional experience. Check them out with friends who've had extensive experience in business.

- Very important basic principle: The right thing to do is also the *smart* thing to do. In business as in the family, the most important thing is trust. Your integrity is your most important asset. Be honest, keep your word, treat your work as service to others, and mind your own business.

- Don't be embarrassed about where you grew up, where you went to school, your physical looks, or anything else you can't change. Generally speaking, if you ignore these things, so will everyone else.

- Measure wealth not by the things you have, but by the things you have for which you would not take money.

- Determine clearly what is really important to you, and then build your life around that.

- Luck is a matter of preparation meeting opportunity.

- The ability to act faster than anyone else can be your greatest professional asset.

- If you really want to do something, you'll find a way; if you don't, you'll find an excuse.

- "One of these days" is really none of these days.

- Excellent performance has two sources: (1) clear focus on goals, and (2) the uncomfortable pressure of deadlines.

- Having trouble with a certain course of action? Doing more of what doesn't work doesn't make it work any better. Consider taking another approach, even if this means starting over from the beginning.

- If you promise something, either do it or explain why you can't.

- Read the company newsletter to stay on top of what's happening in your organization and what your bosses are thinking. Also, when people you respect recommend certain books for professional enhancement, read them. In other words, decide to be constantly learning.

- Dress for the job you want, not the one you have. Let your dress and grooming reflect your self-respect and professionalism. Pay special attention to your shoes and shirts. Your bosses will notice.

- Get in good physical shape and work to stay that way. Generally speaking, conspicuously overweight people suffer a competitive disadvantage in the workplace. Unless they're highly skilled in some technical area, they get passed over in favor of healthier looking competitors, especially if their jobs involve contact with the public. This is often unfair, certainly—but much of life is unfair, and we have to come to terms with reality.

- "Productive time" is time at your desk or workbench, period.

- Deadlines are valuable, for there is such a thing as good stress; we do our best work when under reasonable pressure. In other words, deadlines are the ultimate inspiration; they force us to do what needs to be done.

- Mind your own business. The top of someone's desk isn't a bulletin board, so don't read what's on other people's desks or computer monitors. If bosses or coworkers find you snooping, they won't trust you.

- Similarly, don't make critical comments about matters that lie outside your areas of responsibility. Stick to your own job. Don't get a reputation as a busybody. Every responsible professional knows that loose-talking meddlers are also either slackers or control freaks. In either case, nobody trusts them.

- Don't talk about people behind their backs. If you gossip, you may be doing someone a serious injustice, and people won't confide in you. Besides, office gossip has a mysterious way of reaching the one gossiped about. Here, as in so many other areas, keep your mouth shut and you'll stay out of trouble.

- If there's a lot of bad-mouth gossip in your office, especially about management, start looking for another job. Poor morale nearly always arises from dysfunctional management. A company rife with gossip is most likely on the verge of business collapse.

- Don't take things personally. If some people are ill-tempered or rub you the wrong way, that's their problem—it's usually something in their private lives off the job. Don't let their problem become yours. Just shrug it off and get on with your job.

- Related to this, if you must correct someone, don't get personal about it. Correct the fault, not the person. Make the correction privately, never in front of others.

- Don't let anyone rush you into important decisions. Just say, "I'd like a little more time to think it over." Indicate when you expect to arrive at a decision and then stick to it.

- Friday afternoon is the worst time to talk with anybody about something important.

- Think of the intensity and concentration you put into your work on the last two days before you leave for vacation. Ideally, that's how you should work every day.

- To make your writing flow more easily and naturally, write your first draft as if it were a letter to someone you know. Then go back and shape it as a more formal presentation.

- It's worth investing time to take a public speaking course. Very few people are comfortable giving oral presentations to a group. Therefore, anyone who can do this with a certain professional poise and self-confidence makes a great impression. Being able to think on your feet and express yourself in public is one of the most valuable skills you can master.

- Never send a letter or memo or email that you've written in anger. If you do, you'll probably regret it. Hold it for a day or two, look it over calmly, then either revise it or throw it away.

- Don't ever put anything in writing that could, in the wrong hands, be damaging or embarrassing to you. Documents tend to take on a life of their own; they often circulate in ways difficult, sometimes impossible, to control. This is especially true of emails.

- Never put your signature on anything without first reading it carefully. If you sign something hastily and carelessly, you may wind up needing a lawyer.

- Do not tell racist, ethnic, or sexist jokes. They're hurtful to people and therefore dishonorable. And they can land you in trouble.

- Grudge-bearing is a waste of time and psychic energy. If you spend too much time judging people, you won't get much accomplished.

- Don't use coarse language in the workplace. If you do, people lose respect for you. Consciously or otherwise, people associate habitual foul-mouthed speech with childish self-centeredness or a fundamental lack of self-control.

- Use the company's resources—money, cars, office supplies, travel accommodations, computers, the Internet—prudently and honestly. Take care of them.

Never pilfer anything or pad your expenses.

- Be nice to people who wait on you or clean up after you: janitors, salespeople, waiters, bus drivers, clerks behind a counter. Look them in the eye, smile, and say "please" and "thank you." They're human beings like you, with dignity and feelings, but they seldom receive the courtesy and kindness they deserve.

- Don't whisper with people in hallways or other public places. This looks sneaky and conspiratorial. If you want to have a private conversation, step into a room or out of people's earshot and then talk in a normal voice.

- No matter what it takes, be on time for all business appointments. If possible, arrive a few minutes early. No matter how late you work, get to your job the next day on time.

- Strive your best to meet a deadline, especially one you've promised to meet. If you clearly cannot meet it, apologize and ask for an extension to do the job right. (People won't remember that work was a little late, but they'll remember if it was shoddy.) Once you've gotten an extension, that's it. Do whatever is necessary—stay up late, call in outside help—to turn in good work on time.

- Even better, plan to turn in good work consistently ahead of time. If work is due by 5:00 p.m. on Friday, turn it in by noon on Friday, or even on Thursday. You can't always do this, of course, but it's worth the effort. Your boss will notice.

- When you are seriously vexed by a problem, ask your-self how important it will be a year from now, or six months from now, or even next week. Many things we worry about never happen—and among those that do, about 90 percent are beyond our control anyway.

- Admit your mistakes. Forgive those of others.

- Show appreciation often. Being appreciated is the greatest human need.

CHAPTER 10

Guidelines for Professional Etiquette

Ask anyone in business and professional life and they'll tell you about the great importance of professional etiquette. Though details of business manners seldom appear in writing, they're as vital as good social manners, and they serve the same purpose. They make interpersonal dealings more considerate and gracious. Good professional manners put people at ease and make them feel respected as clients, customers, or fellow workers. All this has a serious impact on a young man's career.

People in the workplace will tell you that some workers, especially young ones or fairly recent college graduates, are clueless about these matters of etiquette. They may be technically skilled but socially clumsy. Bosses and fellow workers may assume, rightly or wrongly, that these young people are lacking in professionalism, or even common sense. That's why committing blunders in these areas not only looks bad but can hurt your career.

The details of professional etiquette that follow will help you form habits of treating people graciously at your workplace—and thereby win their affectionate respect.

If you consult experienced professionals about the items here, they can comment on each point, give some specific examples from their work experience, and even add suggestions of their own. Try it.

General guidelines

- Bear in mind the following definitions of a gentleman: A gentleman is a man who does no harm and gives no offense to anyone on purpose, who is open to friendship and cherishes friends, who sees his work as service to others, who has the grace to disagree without being disagreeable, and who has eyes for the needs of those around him. Strive to become this kind of man.

- Say "please" and "thank you" a lot. Be known as a person who appreciates other people's dignity, rights, feelings, and earnest best efforts. Show appreciation; it's the greatest human need.

- "Thank you" is always an appropriate response to any kind of praise or favor. When at a loss for words to respond to praise, just say "thank you" and let it go at that.

- Keep on hand a supply of good-quality thank-you notecards or "monarch" stationery ($7^1/_4$ x $10^1/_2$), preferably personalized with your name, address, etc. Use these to send a personal handwritten thank-you note immediately (within twenty-four hours) for gifts, job interviews, and substantial favors. This one courtesy can get you very, very far.

- Whenever meeting people after some absence, give your name. Even if you've met the person before, he or she may not recall your name.

- If you're meeting someone for the first time and you didn't understand his or her name, ask the person to repeat it. ("Please forgive me, I didn't quite catch your name.") This isn't awkward or offensive. You show you are sincerely interested in getting the name right and in making the person's acquaintance.

- When speaking with someone, make eye contact. Show that you're interested in that person and what he or she has to say. Never look repeatedly over someone's shoulder to seek out some other, more interesting conversation. This is insulting.

- Be patient with slow talkers. Don't interrupt to finish other people's sentences for them, especially your boss.

- Whether in the office or on social occasions, avoid certain topics in your conversation because they may lead to awkwardness, boredom, embarrassment, or resentment. These topics are (a) your own health or others' health, (b) controversial issues, (c) the cost of items, (d) topics of a sexual nature, (e) personal misfortunes, (f) gossip, (g) stories of questionable taste or dirty jokes, and (h) politics.

- Never use humor that offends: no racist, sexist, ethnic, or crude jokes.

- Don't open conversations by asking people what they do for a living. Though Americans are inclined to do this, for many people the question is awkward, especially if they're currently unemployed. And to foreigners especially, the question seems personally intrusive and therefore rude. Wait and let the person's occupation come up naturally during the conversation. If it doesn't, just let it go.

- Whenever you must send a letter or memo to some-one, make sure you spell the person's whole name correctly. Do whatever it takes to get the right spell-ing: look it up in a directory or online, or make a phone call to someone who knows. People get an-noyed when you misspell their name; they tend to attribute it to unprofessionalism on your part, and they're inclined to discount what you have to say in the rest of your message.

- Don't use the term "Mister" when referring to your-self, either on your stationery or on the phone. Just use your name. The word "Mister" is an honorific term; we use it with others to show respect for them. We don't use it when referring to ourselves.

Social events

- When inviting someone to a social occasion, don't preface your invitation by asking, "What are you do-ing this Friday night?" or "Are you busy this Saturday evening?" This puts people on the spot. Just explain what you have in mind and leave your friends a way, if they prefer, to decline your invitation gently and diplomatically.

- If you receive an invitation that says "RSVP," be aware that it means to let your host know whether you will attend or not. Do this without fail, and promptly. The host needs this information to plan the event's food, seating arrangements, etc., and your negligence here is a real disservice. It's exceptionally ill-mannered.

- Arrive on time. Always be punctual in keeping appointments—even for light social occasions, even with good friends. If you're unavoidably late, try to call ahead; in any case, offer an apology.

- When you're invited to someone's home, try to arrive on the dot, no more than five minutes late. (The exception to this is an event like an open house.) Don't arrive early, though, for your hosts may not yet be ready to receive you.

- Mingle with other guests, not just your friends. Seek out people who seem to be standing alone.

- Don't linger too long in conversation with your host. He or she needs to circulate among the other guests.

- Limit alcohol: one or two drinks maximum. Stick with wine or some nonalcoholic drink rather than hard liquor and learn to nurse one drink throughout the party. Beware of imbibing alcohol on an empty stomach: before you drink, eat some "finger food" so the alcohol will take longer to enter your system and thus keep you in good shape. And of course, never, ever, drink to the point of inebriation.

- Never press an alcoholic drink on someone who declines it. He or she may be unable to drink for religious or medical reasons or may be trying to recover from an alcohol problem.

- Don't eat too much food. The purpose of a social event is to mingle with people and make friends, not to overindulge in food and drink. The people come first and the food and drink are incidental. Don't give people the impression that your priorities are reversed.

- If you're having a business lunch, don't start talking business until everyone has ordered food. Make small talk until the waiter has taken the orders.

- If you're having a meal with fellow workers, avoid shoptalk unless the meal is clearly for business. Don't discuss work. A social occasion is supposed to be a break from work.

- When you meet with professional people socially (especially physicians, accountants, and attorneys), don't put them on the spot by asking for professional advice. If you think those professionals can be of help to you, ask if you can call their office sometime later to make an appointment.

- When you attend social events, always carry a couple of your business cards. But don't offer your card to someone until the very end of a conversation, when you're parting, and then only if it's clear that the new acquaintance might like to meet with you again. Passing out cards gratuitously looks pushy and amateurish.

- Don't be the last to leave, but stay at least one hour.

- Before leaving, be sure to thank the sponsor or host. If you leave along with several other people, it's courteous to call the next day and thank the host personally. If you received a written invitation, it's courteous to write a thank-you note. (The protocol is this: an informal phoned invitation should lead to a phone-call thanks, and a written invitation to a written thanks.)

Telephone etiquette

- Speak in a normal, pleasant, courteous voice, especially when answering. Get into a habit of smiling when you speak.

- When you phone someone you don't know well, identify yourself to whoever answers the call.

- Very important: Before launching into a phone conversation, first ask if this is a good time to talk.

- Try to answer before three rings. Don't ever slam the receiver.

- If you foresee that you might have to leave a voice mail message, have a brief, clear message rehearsed, one that doesn't sound nervously improvised. Always leave your number, even with people who probably know it; you save them the trouble of looking it up. Say the number slowly at the beginning and end of the message.

- Return all phone calls promptly.

- Don't waste people's time with phone tag. Let people know when you'll be available.

- Give people on the phone your undivided attention. Don't make side remarks to someone else in the room or otherwise convey that you're doing other tasks while conversing.

- In the office, limit personal calls to important matters only, and be brief.

- Unless you want people to call you at home or on your cell phone after hours, don't give out your home or cell phone number.

Office etiquette

- When guests enter your office or cubicle, stand to receive them, make eye contact, and give a warm handshake, then gesture to where they may sit. Unless you are both going to look at papers, arrange the seating so you don't have a desk or table between you and them. Give them your undivided attention; don't glance at your watch or otherwise convey that you're impatient for them to leave. When they're leaving, walk them to the reception area.

- Unless you have explicit permission, don't enter your boss's office when he's not there.

- Avoid standing directly behind people sitting at computers.

- Never take something from someone's desk without asking—not even scissors or staplers.

- Don't hang out in the doorway of someone's office or cubicle while he or she is on the phone.

- When you walk into an office or cubicle, remain standing unless invited to sit. Then sit down gracefully and maintain an attentive posture.

- If you're in someone else's office or cubicle and that person receives a phone call, exit gracefully without interrupting the call. Stand up and silently gesture that you'll wait outside.

- Keep office visits businesslike and brief. Be pleasant— but get to the point, get what you need, and then leave.

- Business people these days are deluged with e-mails.

An executive typically receives at least sixty a day. So try to avoid sending unnecessary or multiple e-mails to someone that you know is busy. Before you e-mail, pause to ask yourself: Is this message necessary? Can I hold off a while and combine several points of information into one message? (In order to cut back on e-mail traffic, some offices have a policy to hold off on perfunctory thanks and routine acknowledgments. Find out the policy in your office and stick to it.)

CHAPTER 11

Business Leadership

People tend to become like their model or ideal. A young man starting out in his career should form a vision of what he'd like to become over its course. Not just what he'd like to *do*, but what he'd like to *be*. This is why it's worth studying the lives of people who exemplify professionalism.

Let's look at the traits most commonly found among successful business and professional leaders. What attitudes and actions characterize an outstanding leader, maybe the sort of leader you aspire to become? Think about each of these.

- An outstanding professional leader has a clear, long-term vision of the company's future success, and he communicates this goal, at least occasionally, to everyone who works with him. He thinks several years ahead. This goal-setting drives him and his team forward—he knows that the effectiveness of what people do is enhanced when they're focused on a future achievement.

- A leader encourages and practices teamwork. He looks mostly for *strengths* in people and sees his job as coordinating those strengths toward the team's collective endeavors. He helps his colleagues, especially subordinates, develop their strengths and skills as they carry out clear-cut responsibilities.

- A leader is service-oriented. He knows that professional success means constant delivery of high-quality service. A business works best when it's dedicated to effecting change for the better in the lives of clients or customers, and his job is make this happen effectively and consistently.

- Though he thinks of the future, a leader pays attention to present detail, the nitty-gritty before him. His eye for detail is derived, in fact, from his long-term vision and commitment to service.

- A leader sets priorities and sticks to them. When faced with a problem, he asks, "How important will this be a year from now, five years from now, or later?" Within this framework, he shrugs off or ignores unimportant snarls and minor setbacks.

- A leader knows how to concentrate, to focus entirely on what's before him. He works to eliminate unnecessary distractions.

- A leader tends to see problems as challenges, not just hassles. He has a kind of sporting spirit about his work, and he knows that any sport involves occasional bruises, mistakes, and disappointments. He learns from mistakes, his own and others', and helps his subordinates do the same.

- If resources are scarce, including time, a leader works *smart*. He makes the most of what he has available, including slivers of time here and there. He doesn't procrastinate; papers don't pile up on his desk. He thinks before he acts, then acts intelligently and decisively.

- A leader takes personal responsibility—no excuses, no alibis, no whining, no "victim complex," no shifting of blame. He accepts the consequences of his free decisions and actions, including mistakes.

- When he's unsure what to do, a leader secures the best advice he can and weighs it seriously. Then he acts. Indecision never leads to inaction. His job is to act—that's what he's paid for.

- A leader is conscious of his authority, and comfortable with it. He has rights because he has duties. His knows that his rights come with the job.

- A leader has self-respect and self-confidence, and these traits inspire respect and confidence from others.

- A leader rewards good effort, making praise as specific as blame—and just as sincere. He affirms and encourages his people, pressing them to give their very best regardless of shortcomings. He sees part of his job as keeping obstacles out of his people's way, eliminating whatever holds them back from their best performance.

- When he must correct others, a leader corrects the *fault*, not the *person*. He comes down on the foul-up, not the one who did it. He corrects people privately, never in public. If he goes too far, he apologizes. He puts fairness ahead of his ego.

- A leader is a good listener. When people come to him with problems, he gives them his undivided attention. While listening, he tries to understand them: their motives, their experience (or lack thereof), their needs and uncertainties. He reflects: "Is there a bigger problem underlying this little problem? What is it? How can I help?"

- When a leader thinks about his people's professional development, his frame of reference (consciously or intuitively) comprises the virtues: sound judgment, responsibility, perseverance, self-discipline. He wants and expects his people's effort to grow in these areas. His company depends on it. He knows his business is only as strong as the people who work for it.

- A leader is a professional. He sets high standards for his own performance and does his best work whether he feels like it or not. In a sense, he's strong enough to ignore fatigue, anxiety, or temptations to slack off. He enjoys his top performance; his delight in life comes as much from his work as from his leisured recreation.

- Consciously or otherwise, a leader knows that no ideal becomes reality without sacrificial effort. His high personal and professional ideals, in fact, transform his hard work into a sporting adventure.

CHAPTER 12

Heading Toward Marriage

If God calls you to marriage, you and your fiancée should take seriously what is presented to you in the Church's marriage preparation courses. An immense amount of experience with marriages—some of it sad, even tragic —has gone into what you are taught.

This isn't the place to repeat what these courses normally teach. The points listed below are supplementary ideas that reinforce the standard teaching and, I hope, give you insights to think about. Your marriage is the most serious step you'll ever take. It has lifelong consequences.

- Very many of the happiest and most secure marriages started out as friendship: the couple first knew each other and socialized as friends. They enjoyed each other's company. They liked each other—and over time this friendly affection turned into love.

- Despite what popular culture claims, love isn't just a bundle of sentiments. Love is, rather, the willingness to endure all sorts of difficulty, hardship, tedium, disappointments, and setbacks for the sake of someone else's happiness and welfare. Love is another word for sacrifice and responsibility. Love is the greatest thing in life. In many ways, love is life.

- Blessed John Paul II expressed it this way: "Man cannot live without love. He remains a being that is incomprehensible for himself, his life is senseless, if love is not revealed to him, if he does not encounter love, if he does not experience it and make it his own, if he does not participate intimately in it."[1]

- Therefore, marriage is not a business deal, a 50/50 proposition; it's more like 90/10 or 80/20. Marriage works best when each partner gives generously to the other with little regard for return.

- Look a few years ahead. Someday your growing children, especially in adolescence, will ask you whether your relationship with your wife before marriage was chaste—whether your love for each other was one of Christian purity. They'll also ask whether you lived a chaste life as a single man. Or if they don't ask, they'll certainly wonder. What will you tell them?

- When you're thinking seriously of marrying someone, pay close attention to how she treats her family—parents, brothers and sisters, if any. It's a preview of things to come. How a woman treats the family she comes from is pretty much the way she will treat her husband.

- If you're thinking about marrying a woman who has some defect that troubles you, don't count on her reforming after you're married. This rarely happens. By and large, what you see before marriage is what you get afterwards.

- Marriages are healthy when both spouses work to improve themselves, not each other. When spouses

[1]*Redemptor Hominis*, 10

try to change each other, the result is nearly always trouble. (The obvious exception is helping a loved one overcome alcohol or other substance abuse; this requires relentless love and professional help. But don't enter into a marriage with such a person counting on change later. The change needs to come first.)

• Remember that women are more verbally gifted than men. They express their thoughts and feelings more aptly in words, so verbal expression means a lot to them. For this reason, every man must often express his love for his wife in well-chosen words: "I love you ... You are everything to me ... I will never stop loving you. ..." It's not enough to serve her wordlessly with your deeds, or to assume she knows how much you love her deep down. She needs to *hear the words.*

• Charity means mostly *compassionate understanding.* Some of the most beautiful and loving words in marriage are, "I'm sorry. Please forgive me." Sincere apology strengthens marriages. It enkindles love over and over again, as it does in the sacrament of reconciliation.

CHAPTER 13

Parent-Leaders

As part of preparation for marriage and family life, let's look at the mission and job description of great parents, those valiant men and women who sacrifice and prepare their children to lead a fulfilling life. By way of summary, how would we describe these parent-leaders in action? How do they carry out the adventure of raising a family? This is what we see. . . .

- The husband puts his wife first. In his priorities, her happiness and welfare are his top priority, and his children know this. They know it because he leads them by his own example to love, honor, and obey their mother. If they fail to do this, they answer to him for it. (This is more than half the secret of effective fatherhood: striving to live as a devoted, affectionately supportive husband.)

- The wife puts her husband first. Her husband's welfare and happiness come closest to her heart, and the children know this. In countless small ways, she leads the children to honor their dad. She never belittles or contradicts him in front of the children, for that would undercut his authority and lead the children to disrespect him. She deeply appreciates his loving sacrifices, including his long hours of work, and she shows this. She leads the children to see their father as a heroic man—a pattern for each son's manliness and a model for each daughter's later choice of a husband. Besides, she's canny enough to foresee the future; when the children are adolescents, and too big for her to handle in tight situations, it is Dad who will handle matters more effectively. But this will only work if, by then, the children have a lifelong habit of respecting their father.

- Both parents see themselves as partners in a collective team enterprise. Together they strive to present a united front to the children. They check with each other about decisions, large and small, that affect the children's welfare. They draw on each other's strengths and, in different but complementary ways, they reinforce each other.

- Parent-leaders see all their sacrificial efforts—the rigorous work of parenthood—as an *investment*, not just a vexing hassle. They are investing most of all in the stability and happiness of their children's future marriages, not just their careers. They sense that whatever will make their children great spouses and parents will also lead to success in their careers. Mom and Dad look forward to their later reward, the payback for all their sacrifices: being proud of their grown children and enjoying life with their grandchildren.

- Parent-leaders correct their children's faults, not them personally. They "hate the sin, but love the sinner." They combine correction and punishment with affectionate forgiveness, understanding, and encouragement. They are neither weak nor harsh, but rather *affectionately assertive.* They love their children too much to let them grow up with their childish faults and self-centeredness still intact.

- When they must correct anyone in the family, they do this personally and privately whenever possible. They do not chew people out in public.

- Mom and Dad never fear being temporarily "unpopular" with their children. The children's long-term happiness is more important than their present sulking and bruised feelings from correction. The parents are confident that their kids' resentment will soon pass; someday, please God, the children will understand and thank Mom and Dad for the love behind their steadfast guidance.

- Parent-leaders encourage their children frequently, explaining how to do things right and showing them how to do the right thing. They direct rather than manage, and they make praise as specific as blame.

- Parent-leaders are confident of their authority, which is as great as their responsibility. They know that as parents they have rights over their children, including the right to be respected and obeyed. They will not permit their children to infringe on those rights; in a sense, they're prepared to defend their rights against their children's aggression. And they know that this lesson has lifelong consequences.

- Parent-leaders do not allow electronic rivals in the home to undermine their authority or undo their lessons of right and wrong. They keep the media and Internet under discerning control, allowing only what serves to bring the family together.

- Parent-leaders understand that they must lead their children to *see the invisible*—those critical realities that form a great life: *character, conscience, honor, integrity, spirit of service, truth, justice, moral obligations, social obligations, family solidarity, the soul.*

- Parent-leaders respect their children's freedom and rights. They teach them how to use their freedom responsibly, and they exercise only as much control as the children need. They set limits to the children's behavior. They know they must also show that *invisible line separating right from wrong* in a host of situations—the line we cross when we infringe on the rights of others. This includes the parents' rights not to be disobeyed or treated with disrespect. Within the lines, children are free; outside the lines, others' rights get violated—and this the parents will not permit.

- Mom and Dad share conversation with their children until they and their kids know each other inside out. They go out of their way to listen to their children and pay close attention to their growth in character. They watch over and guide their children's performance in sports, chores, homework, good manners, and relations with siblings and friends. They know what goes on in their home and inside the growing minds of their children.

- Mom and Dad want their children to be active, and they know that all active people make mistakes. They allow their children to learn from their own blunders. They teach them that active life involves sensible risk-taking, including the risk of error, and that there's nothing wrong with mistakes if we learn from them.

- Parent-leaders set aside fatigue, anxiety, and temptations to slack off—putting duties ahead of self-centered pursuits. They set aside the evening news to help with homework. They go without TV to set a good example. They let their kids work with them around the house even when they mostly get in the way. Like a good boss, each parent is always available to help and advise; consequently, children sense that their parents would drop anything if they really needed them. Parents are willing to put off a life of leisure until their children have grown and gone. Now, while the children are still at home, their needs come first.

- Parent-leaders give their children a sense of family history and continuity. They tell stories about grandparents and forebears—people of quiet courage and even heroism.

- Parent-leaders let the children know their opinions and convictions about current events and their likely drift—that is, the future world the kids will have to cope with. They explain, as best they can, the past causes and future implications of present-day affairs. They press their children to become readers as well—to get out of themselves and learn about life through the eyes of others.

- Mom and Dad are open to the children's suggestions, their "input" about family decisions. After all, it's their family, too. When matters are of little weight, the parents accede to the preferences. They let them have their way, or at least let them have their say. But larger, more important matters are decided by the parents. Sometimes, for instance, Mom and Dad will let children choose what dessert to enjoy or what games to play, but the parents decide which school the children attend and which TV programs and websites will enter the house.

- When either parent has caused offense, he or she apologizes. Each puts justice and truth ahead of ego.

- Habitually, parents punctuate their speech, especially toward each other, with *please, thank you,* and *excuse me.* They teach their children to do the same.

- Parent-leaders draw strength and courage from their ethical principles and love for their family.

- Parent-leaders know that time passes quickly and they don't have much of it, so they make smart use of scant resources. They make the time, even small slivers of it here and there, to be with their children.

- Their life as parents is, to them, one of noble, self-sacrificing adventure. As long as the kids are in their care, they will not quit or slacken in their mission to form their children's character for the rest of their lives. No matter what the cost, Mom and Dad will support and provide for each other and for their children. To them, the family is the meaning of their lives, the object of their powers, the center of their hearts.

Children led by parents like this have a fighting chance to become great men and women. They grow to honor Dad and Mom, live by lessons learned since childhood, and pass these on to their own children whole and intact.

CHAPTER 14

Religious Instruction of Your Children

How do you form your children in Christian living and love for God? What do you do to save their immortal souls? How do you foster in your children the infused virtues of faith, hope, and love that they received at baptism? How do you prepare them to receive the indwelling of the Holy Spirit with all his gifts and fruits?

The collective experience of conscientious Catholic parents is as follows.

- Take an active, attentive hand in their catechetical instruction. Bear in mind that your children, years from now, will need to pass on the faith to your grandchildren, and they may need to do this by themselves with little outside support. At that time, they will fall back on the remembrance of your instruction now. You are storing up a memory for them, giving light and example for them to live by later.

- Make prayer a normal, natural part of family life: prayers before meals, in tough situations (illness, upcoming exams, financial problems), and at bedtime (apologizing to God with an act of contrition). Seeing you living happily as a "child of God," your children grasp an important life lesson: prayer is part of grown-up life, not just a charming childhood make-believe that's later outgrown, like Santa Claus.

- Children delight in stories, and they acutely need heroes to pattern their lives after. Tell them stories of Christ and his Blessed Mother and the apostles, figures of the Old Testament, the heroism of the saints and missionaries. (If your children have no heroes, they will pattern themselves after media "celebrities.")

- From time to time, ask your children for their prayers, explaining that God loves children's prayers in a special way. Children can't contribute many big things to family life, but their prayers are powerful before God. Let them see how much you value their prayers, how you and God are grateful for their prayers.

- Lead your children to pray for the Holy Father, for our bishops (successors of the apostles), priests and religious, the needs of the Church (especially vocations), and the needs of everyone, including our public leaders.

- Teach reverence for the Eucharist: dressing well for Mass, genuflecting reverently, preparing for Holy Communion—in short, showing exquisite good manners toward Christ, who is with us as our greatest Friend. Make visits to the Blessed Sacrament just to say hello to Jesus, who is all alone so much of the time.

- Teach your children to have recourse to Mary. The Rosary—or part of it, for small children—is a significant part of family life, a bedrock for the family's faith and hope. Because you earnestly beseech Mary thousands and thousands of times, ". . . Pray for us sinners, now and at the hour of our death," you are confident she will intercede with her Son to grant each of your children a great, adventurous life and a holy death.

- Show them your love for the sacrament of reconciliation. Our Lord said that we must become like little children, and he grants us "spiritual childhood" with each good confession. No matter what wrong we have done, our sincere sacramental apology leads us to begin a new life—to recapture once again all the innocence and purity, the joyful peace of mind, that we knew as children.

- Insist on this flat rule for your home: "We will have nothing in this house that treats other people as mere objects. Therefore, we exclude media presentations—Internet sites, TV, videos, video games, magazines, music lyrics, posters—that glorify pornography (or anything like it), gratuitous violence, coarseness, vulgarity, anything that degrades people and offends God." This you stick with, not just to shield or protect your children, but rather to teach them your steel-hard moral principles and the reasons behind them.

- When your children are adolescents or young adults going out on their own, remind them of what you have taught them since childhood: "Remember, God is always with you. Don't do anything to offend him. We are confident that you will live by our faith and moral principles, and our prayers go with you every day."

- Finally, make clear to your children that the finest way they can honor and thank you, their parents, is to embrace your religious principles, live by them all their lives, and pass them on to your grandchildren as the family's sacred legacy.

As your children approach and grow through adolescence, remember this: Young people aren't looking for a set of rules to live by. What they're really looking for is a life to imitate. They ask themselves, "Who lives a great life? Whom shall I be like?"

If you love your children unconditionally, and if you strive to live a holy, adventurous life, you will win your children's hearts. As the years pass, your heroic, happy life will be the pattern for their own.

By living example and word, teach your children your principled convictions about Christian family life, lessons to be engraved forever in their hearts. What should your children remember all their lives and then pass on to their own children?

• God loves each one of us more than all the fathers and mothers in the world love their children. Christ freely came to live among us and suffered and died for each and every one of us personally, by name. He longs for us to return his love, to love him back, and that's what we try to do.

• The noble ambition of Christian parents is that their children grow to become great men and women, faithful to their parents' principles; that brothers and sisters remain loyal friends for life and rejoin again as a family—together with their own families and friends—forever in heaven. This sacred ideal is worth any sacrifice.

• Christian charity means mostly compassionate understanding, willingness to forgive and forget, letting others off the hook, praying for one's enemies, serving others with our prayers and powers. In short, charity means treating others the same way Christ treats us: *pardoning the unpardonable and loving the unlovable.*

- Jesus pleads with us to forgive offenses, and he blesses those who make peace. Among the most beautiful words in family life are these: "I'm sorry. Please forgive me"... and then from the other, "I forgive you." This form of love is the bond of perfection.

- Nothing, absolutely nothing, is worse than sin. To break our friendship with God—that is, to break ourselves against his loving will—is the worst of all tragedies.

- Next to sin itself, and indeed related to it, the worst mistake in life is not to trust God.

- Children should pass through life knowing that, no matter what happens, there are two places on earth where they can always get another chance: in the hearts of their parents and in the sacrament of reconciliation.

CHAPTER 15

Life of the Spirit: Friendship with God

Up to now, we have looked at some of the main sources of happiness and success in life, an overview of how a young man can immerse himself in his work, his dedication to his loved ones, and his hopes for the future. This final chapter will examine how a life of the spirit—an ambition for holiness—gives a joyful unity to every aspect of a young man's life.

Start with this basic idea: The ancient Greeks noted that happiness in life comes from "the full use of one's powers along lines of excellence." This is obviously true of our physical and intellectual powers, and it's true of our spiritual powers as well. When we direct our soul to the loving service of God, who is the source and sustainer and object of our life, we experience the deepest happiness—a joy that nothing can take from us, a sense of purpose in life, a meaning that suffuses everything we undertake.

Someone wise once noted that one of the greatest mistakes in life is to shoot too low. All around us, multitudes of people, including perhaps our friends, shoot too low in their spiritual lives. They cultivate no ambitions directed at knowing, loving, and serving God and then later joining him in heaven—which is why we have been put here on earth. Instead, they live as though God did not exist, as if life ended with death, as if human beings were mere objects, as if man were nothing but a beast. The results are obvious: a life that ricochets between joyless pleasure and deep despair, a desperate flight from boredom, a melancholy that's never far below the surface of one's fleeting amusements.

We are called by God to be saints. In the pursuit of personal holiness we will find our greatest happiness in life, a sense of mission, a reason for being alive. As the great St. Irenaeus once said, "Nothing gives glory to God as much as a man who is fully alive."

This ambition, living a life of holiness in the middle of the world, was the constant teaching of St. Josemaría Escrivá, the founder of Opus Dei. In the later part of his life, he saw this vision of life ratified through the inspiration of the Holy Spirit during the Second Vatican Council.

What does it mean to live like a saint in the world, a normal man who seeks to know, love, and serve God—what we may call a "secular saint"? Blessed John Paul II explained this rich reality in many ways during his long pontificate. It was one of the cornerstones of his teaching. This is how he explained it to a large crowd of laypeople in 1979:

> Christians are "a royal priesthood, a holy nation" (1 Peter 2:9). All Christians, incorporated into Christ and his Church by baptism, are consecrated to God. They are called to profess the faith which they have received. By the sacrament of confirmation, they are further endowed by the Holy Spirit with special strength to be witnesses of Christ and sharers in his mission of salvation. Every lay Christian is therefore an extraordinary work of God's grace and is called to the heights of holiness. Sometimes, lay men and women do not seem to appreciate to the full the dignity and the vocation

that is theirs as lay people. No, there is no such thing as an "ordinary layman," for all of you have been called to conversion through the death and resurrection of Jesus Christ. As God's holy people you are called to fulfill your role in the evangelization of the world.

Yes, the laity are "a chosen race, a holy priesthood," also called to be "the salt of earth" and "the light of the world." It is their specific vocation and mission to express the Gospel in their lives and thereby to insert the Gospel as a leaven into the reality of the world in which they live and work. The great forces which shape the world—politics, the mass media, science, technology, culture, education, industry and work—are precisely the areas where lay people are especially competent to exercise their mission. If these forces are guided by people who are true disciples of Christ, and who are, at the same time, fully competent in the relevant secular knowledge and skill, then indeed will the world be transformed from within by Christ's redeeming power.[1]

An obstacle to people's understanding and acceptance of this idea—living like a saint in the world—probably comes from a mistaken image and concept of a saint. For many, the notion of a saint conjures up images of men and women dressed in ancient or medieval garb, golden haloes around their heads and levitating off the ground or performing startling miracles. Whatever else may be said of them, they seem drastically different from us. They seem anything but normal.

The reality is quite different. Normal, ordinary lay-people—including you—can live like a saint without

[1] Homily at Mass for the People of God, Limerick, Ireland, October 1, 1979

being odd in appearance or behavior or way of life. In the early Church, nearly all the readers of Paul's epistles were ordinary laypeople like you. Yes, there were many bishops and priests and deacons among them, as Christ intended for his Church, but the rest were ordinary people, baptized Christians, whom Sts. Paul and Peter in their letters routinely called "saints."

Today, as in ages past, saints are needed to transform the world. This is what Blessed John Paul II said:

> There is a need for heralds of the Gospel who are experts in humanity, who have a profound knowledge of the heart of present-day man, participating in his joys and hopes, in his anguish and his sadness, and who are at the same time contemplatives in love with God. For this we need new saints. . . . We must beseech the Lord to increase the Church's spirit of holiness and send us new saints to evangelize today's world.[2]

Let's look at some of the outstanding qualities of modern-day saints, people who try to love and serve God in the world.

Saints are people in love with Jesus Christ.

God loves us overwhelmingly, and he wants us to love him back. This is why Blessed John Paul II said, "Faith . . . is not simply a set of propositions to be accepted with intellectual assent. Rather, faith is a lived knowledge of Christ, a living remembrance of his commandments and a truth to be lived out."[3]

[2] Address to the Synod of European Bishops, October 11, 1985
[3] *Veritatis Splendor* #88

Blessed John Paul also said: "Man cannot live without love. He remains a being that is incomprehensible for himself, his life is senseless, if love is not revealed to him, if he does not encounter love, if he does not experience it and make it his own, if he does not participate intimately in it."[4]

St. Augustine, the great sinner who became a great saint, said this: "To fall in love with God is the greatest of all romances. To seek him, the greatest adventure. To find him, the greatest human achievement."

And in another place, he expressed this prayer of gratitude to God: "I have learned to love you late. Beauty at once so ancient and new! I have learned to love you late! You were within me, and I was in the world outside myself. I searched for you outside myself and, disfigured as I was, I fell upon the lovely things of your creation. You were with me, but I was not with you. The beautiful things of this world kept me far from you and yet, if they had not been in you, they would have no being at all."

Gratitude—it is the basis for all piety.

A saint is deeply grateful to God and therefore humble.

"Be thankful," St. Paul said. And with that admonition, he put his finger on one of the secrets of happiness and holiness. Faith is based on loving gratitude.

How does a sincere and heartfelt gratitude affect the way we live? In several ways.

Gratitude leads us to see God as a father who loves us. It gives a heartfelt personal dimension to our faith.

[4] *Redemptor Hominis*, 10

Gratitude makes us acutely aware that life is a gift. Even the ancient pagans, including our distant forebears, saw life this way, as a mysterious, gratuitous gift from some higher power. Our present age is the first in history where people fail to see life as gift. Today's materialistic neo-paganism seems instead to see life as a meaningless molecular accident, a dance of atoms that chance to fall into the phenomenon we call "life."

Gratitude underscores the evil of sin. We see sin not merely as disobedience to a set of rules but rather as what it really is—a horrific offense to the Father who loves us, an ungrateful rejection of his will and mercy, a heartless turning away from his friendship.

Gratitude makes the Mass come alive for us. We worship God to thank him for everything. The Greek word "Eucharist" means "giving thanks."

Gratitude leads us, and in a certain sense impels us, to heartfelt personal prayer. Seeing our lives enriched by God's blessings, we feel the need to pray. We feel a joyful obligation to express thanks by raising our minds and hearts to our heavenly Father.

Gratitude makes us see our adversities in perspective. All things considered, even with our hardships and setbacks, we enjoy a great life. And we're confident that God, who has showered us throughout life with his gifts, will also give us the strength and means to overcome anything. Christ, who saved us through his suffering, will unite our sufferings with his own for the redemption of mankind, including us and our loved ones.

Saints are conscious of being saved by Jesus Christ, and so they appear to be, and they act with the joy of people saved.

Jesus Christ became man not only to save us from the "second death" but also, in his words, that we "may have life, and have it more abundantly" (Jn 10:10). Christ came to *cure the absence of God in people's lives.*

Jesus lives forever as our Savior, and so we Christians are people conscious of being saved—not only from hell, but also from a life blind to the presence of God, which is life lived in confusion, boredom, and darkness.

Religion, it is said, is an acute awareness of the presence, the power, and the love of God for each of us. A Christian is acutely aware of these things. He is conscious of being saved, and thus he is happy. His life, including his life of work, is filled with gratitude and desire to serve others.

So when we speak of sanctifying ordinary life, including the world of work, what do we mean? How can we understand a holiness that suffuses, enlivens, and gives light to everyday affairs?

Consider it this way.

The pages of the Gospel show how Jesus Christ, with a mere act of his will, cured crowds of wretched people from their dreadful afflictions: blindness, deafness, paralysis, leprosy, and diabolic possession.

Use your imagination to fill out this picture: What happened to each of these people after they were saved? How were their lives changed?

Think about it. The real gift Jesus gave to them and their families was the very thing they had most longed for, *nor-*

mal life. Each of these men and women could now do productive work, form a family, live the same routine daily life as everyone else—but with a great difference.

Conscious of being saved, they felt moved with heartfelt gratitude to God every day for the rest of their lives. From the moment they were cured, they saw all the commonplace things of daily life—family, friends, sight, hearing, work, play, health, education, freedom, peace of mind—as wonderful gifts from God.

They could hold down a job just like everyone else; no more begging. So they found joy in their work, delight in turning their newfound powers to the service of others.

They were profoundly and joyfully apostolic. Their transcendent gratitude led them to intimate love for Jesus Christ, their savior. They would speak of Jesus warmly and enthusiastically to anyone whose lives crossed their own, and they wanted to share with everyone their deep happiness, the "good news" of Christ's love and salvation.

So what does it mean to sanctify everyday life? It means to think and live like these people after they were saved, after they received the precious gift of normal life. It means to be moved by gratitude throughout each day and to share this joy with others.

Saints struggle to live as St. Paul and the other epistle writers urged the first Christians to live.

St. Paul extended words of advice and encouragement to the first Christians, all of them converts to our faith, nearly all of them ordinary working people striving to support their families. His heartfelt thoughts apply as much to us today.

In his letter to the Colossians (3:12–15), St. Paul sketched the Christian life, the way Christ's followers should live and treat each other. Here is a beautiful brief description of how we should live as Catholics today.

> Put on then, as God's chosen ones, holy and beloved, a heartfelt compassion, kindness, humility, gentleness, and patience, bearing with one another and forgiving one another, if one has a grievance against another; as the Lord has forgiven you, so must you also do. And over all these put on love, which is the bond of perfection. And let the peace of Christ control your hearts, the peace into which you were also called in one body. And be thankful.

In the First Letter to the Thessalonians, he said, "For this is the will of God, your sanctification . . . Rejoice always, pray constantly, give thanks in all circumstances; for this is the will of God in Christ Jesus for you" (1 Thess 5:16–22).

In Philippians, he urged the Christians to be "blameless and innocent, children of God without blemish in the midst of a crooked and perverse generation, among whom you shine as lights in the world . . . " (Phil 2:15).

And to the Roman converts, he admonished, "Do not be conformed to this world but be transformed by the renewal of your mind, that you may prove what is the will of God, what is good and acceptable and perfect" (Rom 12:2).

*A saint dedicates his daily work to God—offers it up
in holy sacrifice—and uses it to improve the lives of
others. He unites it with the sacrifice of the Mass.*

What does it mean to sanctify professional work?

It means to live always in the presence of God, to do our
work as Christ would do it, and to deal with others (that
is, with other souls) in a spirit of Christian service, with
concern for both their earthly and eternal happiness. It
means to be both normal and holy at one and the same
time. It means to live all the time, including in our professional work, with the transcendent Christ-centered outlook preached by St. Paul: "In him we live and move and
have our being" (Acts 17:28).

So, to sanctify one's work does not mean just making an
initial offering of our work and then sprinkling the day
with aspirations. It is a matter of *being*, not just doing. It is
not a collection of actions but rather a way of life. Msgr.
Ronald Knox put it this way: "Sanctity is not a work done;
it is a life lived."

A man who tries to sanctify himself through his work
enjoys the indwelling of the Holy Spirit. This indwelling
confers the fruits of the Holy Spirit which characterize the
Christian life, the life of a saint.

The Catechism of the Catholic Church (#1832) speaks of
these fruits. It says, "The fruits of the Spirit are *perfections*
that the Holy Spirit forms in us as the first fruits of eternal
glory. The tradition of the Church lists twelve of them:
charity, joy, peace, patience, kindness, goodness, generosity, gentleness, faithfulness, modesty, self-control, chas-
tity." (This list comes from Galatians 5:22–23.)

In practical terms, how do these twelve perfections show themselves in the workplace? How can we describe someone in an office or factory whose personality is set aglow by the Holy Spirit—someone whose unity of life (the material and the spiritual) gives glory to God? The following is a summary recap of what I have noted before.

- As described in Newman's definition of a gentleman, he "has eyes for the needs of those around him."

- He is both task-oriented and people-oriented. He sees his work as service.

- He works hard.

- He does the right thing whether he's being supervised or not. He works to be of service to his employer.

- He is cheerful and good-humored. He takes his responsibilities seriously, but not himself.

- He shows good manners to everyone, not just to those above him or useful to him. He answers communications promptly.

- If he can't say something good about someone, he keeps quiet; he doesn't gossip or backbite. He minds his own business.

- If he must judge another's work, he does this fairly and without personal entanglements. He sticks to facts. He corrects the fault, not the person, and whenever possible, he corrects people personally and privately.

- He gives people the benefit of the doubt, lets others off the hook, forgives and forgets.

- If people are cross with him, he does not take it personally; he assumes they suffer from some underlying personal problem or are just having a "bad day." He shrugs it off and gets on with his job.

- When he has inadvertently caused offense, he apologizes.

- He does not whine or complain.

- He is a good listener and a good explainer.

- He does not give promises lightly; but when he does promise something, he keeps his word. This includes keeping appointments and meeting deadlines.

- He does his work on time (if not ahead of time) and to the best of his ability.

- He does not proffer advice unless it's asked for.

- He takes a sympathetic interest in people's personal problems but does not meddle. When appropriate, he tactfully extends help.

- He appreciates people's earnest best efforts, and he shows this. He knows that people's greatest need is to feel appreciated.

- If he's an executive, he sees his leadership as a form of service, not ego-gratification. He knows that a real leader has joiners, not followers, and so he leads by example. He makes his people want to outdo themselves, to go beyond what they think they can do.

- When he receives praise, he shares it with those who helped him.

- In business dealings with women, he is consistently respectful and prudent.

- He has a collaborative sporting spirit about his work. He sees setbacks as mere temporary challenges, and he hopes for the future. He is honorably competitive and honorably ambitious.

- He is respected by all who know him for his upright character and professionalism. He is approachable as a trustworthy friend—and this is the basis for his apostolate in the workplace.

Saints form a plan of life to give structure to their ambitions for holiness.

Our Lord himself said this: "Blessed are they who hear the word of God and keep it" (Lk 11:28).

As the Old Testament shows in many places, Jewish people who were faithful to God lived by a set of standard behaviors—in diet, work, pious practices—which kept their faith alive and always before them. Indeed, whenever they neglected these standards, they fell into sin and idolatry. An interior life deepens and flourishes with a set of regular practices that act as a supportive structure. This has ever been the experience of our Church.

So, what habits of service to God should you strive for in the midst of your everyday affairs? What, ideally, should you try to incorporate in your life?

Consider these, all drawn from centuries of people's experience in nourishing personal interior life, a life of holiness:

Holy Mass: Take part in the Holy Sacrifice several times each week, daily if possible. The Mass is the greatest prayer, the only one really worthy of God's acceptance, for it is offered by Christ himself. Offer the Mass for your family and friends and for the needs of the Church; you will do more good with your sacrifice than you can possibly imagine.

Mental prayer: Give fifteen or twenty minutes or more each day to personally conversing with our Lord. Remember, prayer is all-powerful, and God gives peace and confidence to all who lift their minds and hearts to him. Never miss this daily nourishing of your love for God.

Read the New Testament: Put your mind and imagination into the luminous words of the New Testament. See the splendid personality of Christ and how he transformed so many souls, showed such love, and suffered and died to save you from the "second death" to fill your life with the joy of faith, hope, and love.

Devotion to our Lady: A daily Rosary and other prayers to the Mother of God will give you strength to persevere in your resolutions. Like all mothers, Mary is a master of affectionate detail.

Frequent confession: Turn to the sacrament of reconciliation often, weekly or biweekly if possible. You will find again, each time, the peace of innocence regained. And besides, what better example could you give to your children? In the years ahead, they will face serious challenges to the values you've tried to instill in them. Their memory of your frequent recourse to God's forgiveness may mean their own salvation. This is no exaggeration.

Spiritual direction: If you meet with a spiritual director regularly, say once or twice a month, you can sustain and even deepen the spiritual strengths God has granted you in answer to your prayers. Thousands of people have had this experience. This resolution could be the one, in fact, that will strengthen your will to keep the others.

■ ■ ■

In summary, consider how the prophet Micah expressed the ideal for living a great life. He said, "You have been told, O man, what is good and what the Lord requires of you: only to do right, to love goodness, and to walk humbly with your God" (Mic 6:8). So be confident and optimistic as you go through life. Always remember what St. Paul said, "For those who love God, all things work together unto good" (Rom 8:28).